A GUIDE TO

AMERICAN

SPORTS CAR

RACING

a guide to

AMERICAN SPORTS CAR RACING

REVISED, THIRD EDITION

WILLIAM S. STONE

photography by **MARTIN J. DAIN**

Doubleday & Company, Inc., Garden City, N. Y., **1967**

INTRODUCTION TO
THE THIRD EDITION

Two basic changes have become clearly evident since the first edition of this book appeared in 1960.

First, American sports car racing has become increasingly *professional*. Prize money, starting money, lap money—all are as common today as racing itself. At least twenty major professional races are now held here each year. (In 1960 there was only Sebring—and maybe a couple of spotty USAC events.) The line between "gentleman" driver and professional is almost totally erased. Today, drivers step regularly back and forth from pro events to amateur ones.

Second, American sports car racing has become increasingly *international*. The route from the United States to Europe has truly become a two-way street. Europe's best drivers compete here half-a-dozen times a year. And Americans are the rule—not the exception—at Le Mans, the Nuerburgring, the Targa Florio. Look under the tail of an English Lotus, Lola, or Elva sports racer, and it's 10 to 1 you'll see a big American V-8 looking back at you. Look in American rule books—like the SCCA's— and you'll see that many pages are practically carbon copies of the Federation Internationale de L'Automobile. And FIA is just a shorter way of spelling European.

This third edition mirrors both of these changes. And blends them into a purpose which has remained unchanged from that of the first edition: to introduce the sport in the United States as a whole.

This is still a book about *sports cars*—not lakesters, dragsters, stock cars, Grand Prix cars, or Indianapolis cars. It's still a book about sports car *racing*—not about rallying, touring, dragging, or record-hunting. It's still

6

about sports car racing in the *United States*—not at Monza or Spa or Monte Carlo.

And it's still a survey, not a mining operation. If you want to dig deeper—and this edition, like the first, is meant to make you want to—try some of the books listed at the end of this one. Or any enthusiast will be flattered to guide you to some of his favorites.

So many people have helped with this book that it's simply impossible to list them all by name. By far the largest group to whom thanks are owed are those who head America's growing number of road-racing courses. The maps, information, and photos they supplied about their particular bailiwicks were absolutely invaluable in the preparation of the section on U.S. courses. A second group who helped enormously were SCCA people—regional officers, people from headquarters, just plain members. Their's were strictly labors of love, and as such, much appreciated.

Thanks are due too to Bill Hughes, who helped get this whole project started. And finally, to Erika, Michael, and David Stone, to whom a new edition means mainly a clacking typewriter, late meals, and an often preoccupied husband and father.

WSS

PHOTO CREDITS

Warren Ballard, pp. 108, 109, 163, 173, and 197; Tom Burnside, p. 185; Daily Leader, p. 193; Daytona International Speedway, p. 164; Irving Dolin, pp. 121, 126, and 189; Robert E. Fields, Jr., p. 181; Ford of Britain, (top) p. 118; Ed Horne, p. 183; Sports-Pix Illustrated photo by Lutzo, p. 175; Gunter Mohr, p. 179; Barbara Nyland, p. 131; Cal Club Photo by George Robitschek, p. 187; Elgin Smith, p. 169 (lower); Strain's Studio, p. 169 (upper); the author, pp. 33, 42, 47, 68, 69, 72, 87, 102, 113, 124, 127, 138, 171, and 199.

CONTENTS

8

CONTENTS

WHAT GOES ON HERE?

Chapter 1

TWENTY FAST YEARS

The first hint comes when the little red Alfa scoots by you on the parkway—top down, roll bar up, big white "29's" on its flanks and tail. Then you pull along side a roaring tower of a trailer truck. Above your head, a scarlet-enameled horse prances on a yellow medallion. Ferraris! At the Highway Diner, two MG's, a Triumph, and a Morgan have pulled up for coffee. You pass again— this time, past a silver Porsche, trailered by a beat-up station wagon crammed with parts and people.

No question about it—today is a race day!

Pull in now at the gate of Lime Rock or Meadowdale or Riverside. Pay for your admission. Park—in a lot crowded with more shapes and makes and sizes of automobiles than Detroit ever dreamed of. Find yourself a good watching spot, and settle down to watch prerace practice. This is going to be a good day.

Not so long ago—say twenty years ago—this kind of a day was almost unheard of in America. Riverside, Lime Rock, Meadowdale, and Daytona weren't even in existence as sports car courses.

The Austin-Healey, the Lotus, the Elva, the Corvette Sting Ray, and the Cobra had never been seen—in this country or anywhere else. America had only the skimpiest supply of sports car racing drivers.

A Little History

The postwar forties gave birth to American sports car racing. What happened in those years was largely the result of a fortunate juxtaposition of factors—of men, of materials (both cars and courses), and of interest in the sport.

For decades there have always been men who were interested in sports cars and sports car racing in this country. But it was an organization of some of these men in the mid-forties that started racing on the road to its current popularity. The organization was the SCCA—the Sports Car Club of America—founded in 1944 by seven men in the area around Boston. Sports cars were a rare breed in America in those days—remember, the war was still on—and it was not for several more years that racing activities could really begin. (Sports cars were so rare in the mid-forties that a member of the SCCA was required to notify the membership if he intended to sell his car—in order to give members first chance at it.)

But sports cars became less scarce as the war ended and European assembly lines returned to peacetime production. Many Americans had had their introduction to sports cars overseas, and had been impressed by them. Then, in the late forties, two sports cars appeared on the American scene that were really to kindle the sports car spark. One was the now-famous British MG-TC—a small, mass-produced sports car that was a barrel of fun to drive but didn't take a barrel of money to own. Its price was right (starting at $2400, it was soon reduced to $1900), and it was durable, reasonably fast for its size, and available. Best of all, it *looked* like a sports car! The second car was the now equally famous Jaguar XK-120. It was a big, powerful, fast automobile that sold at a price far below any at which such a combination of sporting characteristics and performance had ever been sold before. The MG-TC was a fun car, gutty and willing, but far from being a great performer. Its top speed was not much over 75 mph. But the XK-120 was a car that could show its heels to almost anything Detroit produced. And did. It cost less than $4000—and mass production made it available.

If the MG-TC and the XK-120 helped make more and more Americans conscious of the sports car, so did the races organized in the late forties and early fifties. In 1947 the SCCA held its first race meeting at Thompson, Connecticut. In October 1948 the first road race was held at Watkins Glen in Upstate New York. Road racing was revived at

One of the cars that started it all—the XK-120 Jaguar—leads an Austin-Healey through a tight corner.

Bridgehampton, Long Island, in 1949, where it had been absent since the early twenties.

Both the Watkins Glen course and the Bridgehampton course were laid out on town roads. This was true open road racing. At Watkins Glen the pits and a straightaway were smack in the middle of town. This potentially dangerous situation became even more so as both crowds and entrance lists increased. Injuries to both spectators and drivers occurred, and the need for closed, perfectly controlled circuits became more and more evident. But closed road courses require hundreds of acres and hundreds of thousands of dollars to build . . . and the sport still did not command that kind of support.

Fortunately the possibilities of another type of course were rapidly being exploited. This was the airport course. A sizable number of airfields—many of them World War II leftovers—were put to good use as artificial road courses were laid out on their surfaces, staked out by pylons, and flanked by hay bales. Airports like those in Palm Springs, Cal., Linden, N. J., and Sebring, Fla., were pressed into service. The airport course was and is inferior to the road course in the important qualities of diversity and interest. But because crowds can be closely controlled, and good spectator visibility afforded, the airport course was and will probably continue to be an important part of the American sports car racing scene. The most important sports car race in the United States, Sebring, is run on a course that is mostly airfield. Airfields in Stuttgart, Arkansas, Cumberland, Maryland, and Santa Barbara, Cal., are the scenes of many exciting races. But as the sport has

The airport course—flat, broad, artificial.

become more and more popular, an increasing number of closed road courses have been built, until today there are more than thirty of them across the U.S. Sports car racing has fostered these courses, and in turn, the courses have fostered racing. Clearly a course that can be used every day of the year encourages more racing than one that can be opened but once or twice a year.

A somewhat more recent phenomenon that has brought American sports car racing to its present state of health has been the boom in small imported economy cars. Many a small-car buyer who wanted nothing more than cheap, compact transportation has found himself quickly seduced by the sports car characteristics of his small import: its quick steering, good brakes, useful gearbox and outstanding agility. From a Volkswagen or Fiat or Saab it's been only a short step to a Porsche, an MGA, or Alfa for many Americans. And the desire to

The closed road circuit duplicates open roads perfectly, offers a far greater degree of safety.

watch the bigger, racing relations of their economy sedans has doubtless waxed in the hearts of many bug owners who don't have large enough means (or perhaps not small enough families) to make owning a true sports car practical.

American sports car racing has come a long way in twenty years . . . starting from almost nowhere. How far? The thirty closed sports car courses—like Thompson, Conn., Road America, and Laguna Seca— have already been mentioned. All of them built within the last twenty years—most of them within the last ten. Plus, of course, the fifty-odd airport and once-or-twice-a-year circuits in the country. Licensed racing drivers? Add the holders of competition licenses issued by the United States Automobile Club, the Sports Car Club of America, and a number of small amateur clubs around the country, and you've got a group of competition drivers running close to ten thousand. Spectator attendance? It's hard to tell exactly. But the author's personal estimate is that several million spectators make their way to sports car races every year. That's a pretty healthy number of admirers for a twenty-year-old sport. And the number grows each year.

Who Organizes Racing?

Somebody had to organize this booming sport . . . and a number of somebodies have. Just as baseball has its leagues to set up rules, determine championships, keep games from conflicting with one another, and say who is and who is not eligible to play, so the ground rules of sports car racing have been laid down by a number of different organizations. Let's take a look at them.

The organization that lays down the law on all *international* motor sports is the FIA—Fédération Internationale de l'Automobile. Which means that if a driver wants to be recognized as a *world* champion, he must race and win in certain specified events that abide by FIA rules— events that are so recognized (sanctioned) by the FIA. The same goes for a manufacturer who wants to have his cars acknowledged as official international champions.

In racing matters, the United States is represented in the FIA by the Automobile Competition Committee of the United States (ACCUS). The Committee is composed of several individual members, plus representatives of a number of racing organizations: the National Association for Stock Car Auto Racing (NASCAR), the United States Automobile Club (USAC), the National Hot Rod Association (NHRA), and the SCCA.

Which makes the SCCA the big gun in U.S. sports car racing. It is the only member of ACCUS who is seriously concerned with sports car racing, and thus, through ACCUS, it is U.S. sports car racing's voice in the FIA. Not coincidentally, the SCCA's rules and regulations each year bear an increasingly strong resemblance to the rules of the FIA—even those rules which affect SCCA events of a purely local nature.

Every organization that sanctions racing, be it FIA, SCCA, USAC, or local club, is concerned with four primary problems:

1. the conditions under which racing shall be conducted
2. the qualifications and licensing of drivers
3. the classification of racing events
4. the classification of cars.

Racing conditions include such matters as safety regulations, track communications, officials, method of starting cars, flags to be used, insurance, timing and scoring procedures, and a host of other questions . . . the answers to which must be carefully thought out to keep racing reasonably safe, orderly, and uniform.

Driver qualifications is a second important area with which racing organizations must concern themselves. Obviously not everyone who might want to drive in a race can be allowed to do so. Something has to be done to keep the greenhorn in his first MG off the track until he has proved that he can drive safely in competition. So organizations like the FIA, the SCCA, USAC, and local clubs issue competition licenses and require that everyone driving in their races hold such a license. The competition license is simply proof that its holder has competed in a certain number of races, knows the rules, and will not be a menace to other drivers in the race.

Race classification is the third important function of groups that sanction races. Are the races to be local, national, or international? Are they to be professional, amateur, or open to both? The sanctioning organization must decide. At present, sports car races in the United States are broken down into five major classifications:

FIA International Races. This is the top category—races which are on the FIA international calendar in which all FIA-licensed drivers may compete. Prize money is always awarded. Several of these FIA International races held in the United States each year count toward the International Championship: the 12 Hours of Sebring, the Daytona Continental, the Bridgehampton Double 500. Such races are by all odds the most important in the United States—attracting top drivers and factory teams. Second to these races in importance are the several Internationals not included in the championship series: the Times Grand Prix at Riverside, the Monterey Grand Prix at Laguna Seca, and others.

FIA National-Open Races. These events are open to holders of FIA competition licenses. There is one exception: a small group of absolutely top drivers (whose names are published annually by the FIA) are barred, except when the race is held in their own country. Prize money is awarded.

Ooops! Even the pros can get out of control. With an inexperienced driver, such goofs can be a real menace to others on the course.

National-Open races in the United States are primarily those which make up the series known as the United States Road Racing Championship (USRRC). This series of some ten or twelve races (held at courses from coast to coast) was started in 1963, and has proved immensely popular. It is the most important purely national sports car racing in the United States. Cars are modified sports cars, rather than production models, and race in two classes: under 2 liters and over 2 liters.

SCCA National Races. These are amateur races for trophies only. Each of the SCCA's geographical divisions runs a series of these National races each year. Divisional champions meet at the end of the season in a single interdivisional championship event to determine the national championship. Cars compete in both SCCA production and modified classes, as well as other current SCCA-recognized classes (Formula Vee, etc.). These races are only open to holders of SCCA National Competition licenses.

SCCA Regional Races. These are the SCCA's most modest amateur events. They are open to all holders of SCCA Regional Competition licenses, and also to holders of SCCA National licenses who live in the SCCA Division in which the Regional race is held. Any one of the SCCA's one hundred or so Regions may conduct regional races.

At least 95 per cent of the sports car races held in this country fall into one of these five classifications. Events which do not will be local club events of a purely amateur nature.

The Displacement Classes

If racing is to be a sport and not a shambles, some sort of classification of cars must be set up. There would be no more sport in racing Fiats against Ferraris than there would in racing ponies against Percherons. Ponies belong in the pony class, horses in the horse classes. So the third major task of the organizations that sponsor and sanction sports car racing has been to classify the cars that race. But how? On the basis of weight? Of size? Of price? Of horsepower?

The most workable system of classifying sports cars—and the one that is internationally accepted—is based on *engine displacement.* Roughly speaking, the displacement of an engine is the total volume of space in its cylinders. Put it another way: it's the amount of liquid it would take to fill completely the volume displaced by the movement of the pistons in all the cylinders of a given engine. This volume might be measured in pints or quarts, but it is not. It may be measured in cubic inches, as it is in American cars (hence the 396-cubic-inch Corvette engine). But in the case of sports cars the volume is measured in cubic centimeters (cc.) or liters (1000 cc.)—simply because most sports cars are European and Europe is on the metric system. A liter, by the way, is roughly the size of a quart—about 10 per cent larger, to be more exact.

Classification by displacement makes sense. Gasoline engines are powered by explosions. The size of the explosion (and hence the amount of power delivered) is determined by the amount of explosive used. And the amount of explosive (in the case of the automobile, gasoline/air mixture) is governed to a considerable degree by the cylinder's size or displacement. In addition to its reasonableness in terms of physics the displacement system has a practical advantage. Displacement is a factor easily measured, and not as debatable as price, as easily alterable as weight, or as difficult to determine as horsepower. Moreover, it encourages the development of extremely efficient engines—engines that turn out a maximum amount of power for their size.

In 1966, the FIA set up a group of thirteen different displacement classes for sports and touring cars:

Class 1 . . . . not over 500 cc.   Class 8 . . . . 1300 to 1600 cc.

Class 2 . . . . 500 to 600 cc.   Class 9 . . . . 1600 to 2000 cc.

Class 3 . . . . 600 to 700 cc.   Class 10 . . . . 2000 to 2500 cc.

Class 4 . . . . 700 to 850 cc.   Class 11 . . . . 2500 to 3000 cc.

Class 5 . . . . 850 to 1000 cc.   Class 12 . . . . 3000 to 5000 cc.

Class 6 . . . . 1000 to 1150 cc.   Class 13 . . . . above 5000 cc.

Class 7 . . . . 1150 to 1300 cc.

These are the classifications that have international standing in sports car racing.

The FIA recognizes another distinction among sports cars in addition to differences in engine displacements. This is the *purpose* for which the car is intended. And this is an indispensable distinction . . . because it goes as far as is humanly possible to eliminate gross inequalities in racing. If sports cars were rated on displacement alone, the Austin-Healey 3000 would race against the 3-liter Ferrari GT. Yet the Austin-Healey is designed as a well-mannered touring sports car that can also be raced. It is mass-produced by the thousands, and sells for a relatively low price—less than $4000. The Ferrari GT, on the other hand, is designed and built for one purpose only: racing. It's highly tuned, no expense is spared in its building, and it's priced accordingly—well into five figures. On the race track, of course, the Ferrari can run rings around the Healey.

So, to keep things sensible, the FIA has set up seven separate groups of cars with each of the displacement classifications. Here they are:

1. Series Production Touring Cars. A manufacturer must produce at least 5000 of a particular model in one year for it to fall in this category. It may be only very slightly altered from its stock or showroom condition. Permissible modifications include new brake linings, different spark plugs, distributor, shock absorbers, and tires other than those normally fitted by the manufacturer. Alternate gearing and rear-axle ratios are allowed. Four seats are required in all series-production touring cars (except those with engines smaller than 700 cc.)

2. Touring Cars. At least 1000 models must be manufactured within one year. Again, these must be 4-seaters (except under 700 cc.). The modifications allowed to Series Production Touring Cars are also allowed in this group. In addition, cylinder head, valve train, pistons, camshaft, muffler, and brakes may be modified. Any make or size of carburetors may be used. The engine may be internally polished and/or balanced to improve performance.

3. Grand Touring Cars. Only 500 per year need be built, and these need be only 2-seaters. All modifications permitted to Series Production Touring Cars and Touring Cars are permitted in Grand Touring Cars.

4. Sports Cars. These are cars which are almost wholly designed for racing. Two seats are required, and fifty cars must be built per year. All fifty cars must be identical in many respects: bodywork, wheelbase and track, number of cylinders, type of valve gear, bore and stroke, suspension, braking system. Ignition system, carburetors, and manifolds may be altered from car to car. Minimum weight limits are established—ranging from approx. 990 pounds for cars with engines of less than 500 cc. to approx. 1650 pounds for cars of 5000 cc. or over.

5. Special Touring Cars. These are greatly modified versions of Series-Production Touring Cars or Touring Cars. Any cylinder head, engine sump, braking system, or gearbox may be used. Body, wheelbase, track, and general design of the basic car must be retained . . . but other than that, the sky is almost the limit. No minimum number need be built.

6. Prototype Sports Cars. Nominally, these cars should be prototypes for future production, but in point of fact their specifications cover just about any "one-off" two-seater. These are wild ones—highly tuned specials built to do nothing but win races.

7. Two-seater Racing Cars. The very wildest and least restricted of all the two-seater classes. They must run on "pump" gas, have self-starters, a dual braking system, headlights and taillights, and meet certain specifications as to minimum door and seat sizes. Beyond that, almost anything goes.

These, then, are the FIA classes and categories in which sports cars compete, both overseas and in FIA competition in the United States. In SCCA amateur competition, however, a different set of classifications is in effect. In such competition, four categories of cars are commonly raced: *Production, Modified, Formula SCCA,* and *Formula Vee.*

Under SCCA rules, at least five hundred of a given model must be produced for it to qualify as a production car. Certain modifications (see p. 94) are approved. The SCCA, however, does not classify production cars by the time-honored method of engine displacement. Since 1960, the SCCA has grouped cars by their competitive ability—their *relative performance*—regardless of engine size.

For amateur racing, the SCCA system makes extremely good sense. It insures tighter races. It has made a much larger number of cars truly competitive. It holds down the cost of racing for the amateur—by keeping his car competitive no matter what high-priced newcomers arrive in his displacement class. Cars don't become "outdated" as quickly under this system—they just drop a class or two. Here are the SCCA Production Classes for 1966:

Class A Production
 Abarth-Simca 2000
 Cobra (289 or 427 cu. in. Ford V-8)
 Corvette Sting Ray (396 or 427 cu. in. engine)
 Ferrari 250 GTO
 Griffith 200
 Porsche 904

Class B Production
 Aston Martin DB4, DB4-GT, DB4-GT Zagato, DB5
 Corvette (327 or 283 cu. in. engine)
 Corvette Sting Ray (327 cu. in. engine)

Ferrari GTB, Lusso, 250 GT, and 2+2
Jaguar XK-E
Lotus Elan
Mercedes-Benz 300SL
Mustang 350 GT
Sunbeam Tiger (Ford V-8)

Class C Production

Abarth-Simca 1300
Alfa Romeo GTZ
Elva Courier (Mark III and IV; 1800 cc.)
Ginetta G4 1500
Lotus Super Seven
Morgan Super Sport
Osca 1600 GT
Porsche Carrera (1500 and 1600 cc.)
Porsche 2000 GS
TVR (Mark III, 1800 cc., and Climax)

Class D Production

A. C. Ace and Aceca Bristol
Alfa Romeo Giula Spider Veloce, 2600 Sprint and Spider, Giula Sprint
   GT, Giula Sprint Speciale
Arnolt-Bristol
Austin-Healey 3000
Daimler SP250
Elva Mark IV (Ford engine)
Fairthorpe Electron
Fiat-Abarth 1000 (DOHC)
Ginetta G4 1000
GSM Delta
Jaguar XK120, XK140, XK150, XK150S
Lotus Elite
Marcos GT 1000
MGB
Porsche 911
Speedwell Sprite SGT
Triumph TR4, TR4A
Turner-Climax, Turner 1500
TVR Mark III (1622 cc.)
WSM GT

Class E Production

Alfa Romeo Giulietta Sprint Speciale and Zagato, Giulietta Super
    Sprint and Spider, Giula Sprint and Spider
Alpine A 110
Austin-Healey 100-4 and 100-6
Elva Courier, Mark I, II, III and IV, (1622 cc.)
Fairthorpe Minor
Lotus 7 and 7A
Morgan Plus 4 and 4/4 Mark V.
Porsche 912, Super 90, 1600SC and earlier 1500's and 1600's
Renault Alpine A-180-1000
Sabra Sport

Class F Production

Alfa Romeo Giulietta Sprint and Spider
Datsun SPL 311
Fiat-Abarth 700, 750 DOHC and 1000 Monomille
Glas GT 1300
Mercedes-Benz 230SL
MGA Twin Cam
MGA (1500, 1600, and 1622 cc.)
Sunbeam Alpine and Alpine Harrington
Triumph TR2 and TR3
Turner 950S
Volvo P1800

Class G Production

Austin-Healey Sprite (Mark I, II and 1100)
Datsun SPL 310-U
Deutsch-Bonnet (851 and 954 cc.)
Fiat 1500 and 1500 DOHC
Honda S600
Matra-Bonnet MB8S
MG Midget (948 and 1100 cc.)
Morgan 4/4, Mark IV
Porsche 1300 and 1300S
Rene Bonnet CRB/1
Triumph Spitfire

Class H Production

Austin-Healey Sprite (948 cc., limited options)
Fiat-Abarth 850S, 750GT and 750 MM

Fiat 1200 Spider
MG-TC, MG-TD, MG-TF and TF-1500

Sports cars that race in the SCCA Modified classes must indeed be sports cars: carry complete road equipment—headlights, a horn, battery, and self-starter, and be able to carry a passenger. But almost all cars that race in the modified classes are primarily racing cars, rather than dual-purpose mass-produced sports cars. For more discussion of the dual-purpose sports car *vs.* the racing sports car see Section II.

The SCCA Modified displacement classes are:

> Class H . . . . not over 850 cc.
> Class G . . . . 850 cc. to 1150 cc.
> Class F . . . . 1150 cc. to 1600 cc.
> Class E . . . . 1600 cc. to 2000 cc.
> Class D . . . . 2000 cc. to 3000 cc.
> Class C . . . . over 3000 cc.

Supercharged cars must compete one class above that in which their displacement falls. For example, while an unsupercharged modified 1600 cc. car races in Class F, a *supercharged* modified 1600 cc. car must compete in Class E. (The FIA's allowance for superchargers is less generous. Under FIA rules, the displacement of an engine fitted with a supercharger must be multiplied by 1.4 to determine the car's class—an effective jump of *two* classes.) Neither regulation is very meaningful, however, since supercharged engines are rarely seen in sports car competition.

The SCCA also requires that production and modified cars carry both numbers and class letters. Thus the marking "27FP" on the sides of a car mean that it is car #27, racing in the F Production Class. If the marking is "FM" instead of "FP," the car is a modified one.

Formula SCCA cars are not sports cars at all, but single-seater open-wheeled racing cars. They must carry self-starters, be unsupercharged, run on pump fuel, have reverse gears, and be over a specified minimum weight. They are divided into three classes by engine size:

> Class A . . . . . . 1600 to 3000 cc. (Min. Wgt. 1105 lbs.)
> Class B . . . . . . 1100 to 1600 cc. (Min. Wgt. 848 lbs.)
> Class C . . . . . . up to 1100 cc. (Min. Wgt. 750 lbs.)

Like Formula SCCA cars, Formula Vee cars are anything but sports cars. Yet they are distinctly road-racing cars, and hence their adherents are to be found primarily in sports car circles. The formula was first included in SCCA competition in 1964, as a supremely inexpensive class of single-seaters.

Formula Vee cars are based strictly on Volkswagen engines and components with only very limited modifications admitted. A minimum weight of 825 pounds is specified. The following VW components are incorporated, in virtually stock form:

> Front suspension
> Steering gear
> 15″ VW wheels
> 1192 cc. VW engine
> VW transmission and rear axle
> VW brakes

Formula Vee frames must be of tubular steel, and body dimensions are very strictly limited. The cars have become tremendously popular, both because of their low cost ($2500 complete, much less in kits), and because the performance of individual cars is so close that driver skill is extraordinarily emphasized.

The various displacement classes may seem unnecessarily complex. Complex they may be, but unnecessary they are not. They equalize cars within classes so that more of the burden of winning falls on the driver than on the car. In addition, the classes encourage the manufacture and ownership of cars other than those of the superlarge, superpowerful, superexpensive variety. Certainly racing in which only $15,000 Ferraris could win would be good for neither the sport nor the industry.

Chapter 2

AROUND THE COURSE

The black flag is out. Practice is over for E Production cars. One by one, drivers raise a hand to show they're leaving the course and swing off. Porsche . . . Porsche . . . Healey . . . Porsche . . . Elva, Elva, Elva. It's quiet on the track now. From the paddock you can hear the snorts of cars warming up for the next practice session. You stand up . . . brush off the seat of your pants. This seems like a good time to take a good look at the course. You head down toward the start/finish line. . . .

The start/finish line is almost always located on a level straightaway, rarely on an inclined section, never on a curvy "S." There's a good reason for this: visibility. For when a car leaves its pit after a stop, the driver must be able to see some distance back up the course before re-entering it. So must the official who gives him the go-ahead. It's the only way to avoid possible collisions with cars already at speed on the course. Moreover, the timers and scorers at the start/finish need some visual warning that the cars they're keeping track of are about to pass.

Grouped closely around the start/finish line are pits, paddock, timing stand, communications, and official headquarters. "Pits" and "paddock" are a couple of words sometimes confused even by those who should know better. Let's get them straight. Strictly speaking, the "pits" are an area along the edge of the course that is home base for the cars *during the race.* Here the car is refueled during the race, mechanical adjustments or repairs made, tires changed. It is from the pits, too, that instructions are given to the driver by his pit crew (via signs or blackboards) during the course of the race. The pits draw their name from the way they are constructed at many European courses. There they may often be a string of roofed-over concrete pits opening onto the course.

The paddock, on the other hand, is a larger area, close to the course, that opens onto it through one or more short entrance roads. It is the paddock area in which cars are unloaded from their trailers, most pre-race preparations made by drivers and mechanics, and to which the cars return after the race. Except during the race itself, the paddock is home base for cars and crew. Frequently the paddock is also used to line up cars for the race that follows the one in progress. Sometimes this is done on a "false grid"—a replica of the actual starting grid laid out in the paddock. While spectators are never allowed in the pits, at many courses they may purchase passes that allow them to circulate through the paddock. Part of the confusion between pit and paddock results from the fact that the entire pit/paddock area is referred to as "the pits" at some courses. But since their functions are largely separate, the two areas should be properly distinguished.

Near the starting line, and directly on a line with it, is the *timing stand*. It's set up high, so that nothing interferes with its view of the track. In it, during the course of the race, sit timers and scorers, equipped with stop watches and lap sheets. The timers and scorers are assigned one or more cars to watch during the race. Their job is to count the number of laps "their" cars have made and record laps, lap times, and total times for "their" cars. The timing/scoring job is a vital one. For no single judge could keep track of a race. Every car must be checked individually throughout the race. A simple example shows why:

Cars A and B are speeding around the course. A is ahead of B—say two hundred yards. Now B, somewhere out of sight on the back stretch spins off the track. Naturally it takes him some time to get back on the track. But while he is maneuvering his way out of the sand and tall grass, A continues on his way around. So far around, in fact, that he is only two hundred yards behind B when B finally regains the track. For one reason or another, A may be unable to move ahead of B again. So that's the way they cross the finish line—B ahead of A.

Now if there had been only these two cars in the event, it would have been easy for any judge to see that A had passed the timing stand alone at one point, and thus to know that B was actually almost a full lap

One of the jobs of the crew in the
is checking the lap time of their

The timing/scoring stand . . . where the slip of a pencil or the click of a watch can cost a driver a hard-won race.

behind at the finish. But there are often twenty or thirty or more cars in a race, rarely fewer than ten. The cars get completely scrambled during a race of any length. So each car must be individually timed, its laps recorded, and its real (not apparent) position at the finish ascertained. That's the job of timers and scorers.

Racing Officials

Also at the starting line are the race officials: race chairman, chief steward, chief starter, course marshal, flag marshal, chief timer and scorer, communications chief, course physician. These officials are usually supplied by the club or organization that sponsors the race. They have sharply defined responsibilities. Let's look at them:

The *race chairman,* or *race director,* is over-all boss of the entire event. He's in charge of everything except the actual conduct of the race.

The *chief steward* is directly responsible for the conduct of the race. He is supreme authority on all racing matters . . . communications,

re-race preparations in the paddock.

safety, flagging, starting. He decides when the race will begin, and under what conditions it can or must be continued, slowed, or stopped. Nearly all of the other race officials report to him and are responsible to him. They include:

The *chief starter,* who starts the race. When his green flag drops, the race is on. Before the race begins he may also give the drivers other signals: "start your engines" (a "wind 'em up" gesture with his hand), or "one minute to go" (a raised index finger). He is responsible for seeing that cars are lined up in their proper starting order on the grid. During the race he may act as a flagman at the start/finish line, acting under the chief steward's orders. And when his black-and-white checkered flag finally swings down, it does so over the winning car. As other cars follow the winner across the line, they get the checkered flag too. To all drivers it says, "You have completed the race. Take one additional lap at reduced speed." This final lap is the so-called "safety lap"— ensuring that cars will not be a lap short of the correct number if it is later discovered that an error has been made in scoring.

The *course marshal,* or *clerk of the course.* He is responsible for the physical condition of the course itself, making innumerable tours before and between races to check for spilled oil, loose sand on the pavement, misplaced hay bales and pylons, spectators where they shouldn't be, and the like. Until the chief steward has received the course marshal's assurance that the course is clear, no race can begin.

The *chief pit steward,* who is responsible for order in the pits, and for seeing that pit regulations are enforced.

The *flag marshal* and *communications chief,* who together are responsible for the network of flag (or control) stations around the course. The flag marshal is in charge of the flagmen at the stations; the communications chief is in charge of men and equipment that are part of the communications system that links the stations.

The Flag Station

Racing is, of course, a dangerous business. The unexpected often happens. And if the unexpected occurrence is invisible to the drivers,

An indispensable third of the flag station crew—the communications man.

accidents—tragic accidents—can happen. Imagine yourself a driver—barreling into a blind turn at fifty or sixty miles an hour. Halfway through the turn you see that another car has spun and is stalled across the track not more than fifty feet ahead of you. It's hard for anything *but* an accident to happen. It's just this kind of accident—the accident that a *warning* can prevent—that is the job of the men at the flag stations to prevent.

Between them, the flag stations on any given course have a clear view of every inch of the track. On some longer or particularly curvy courses it may take some twenty or more flag stations to do the job. But there's never any skimping on flag stations . . . they're too important. Let's take a look at one.

It takes a bare minimum of three men to run a flag station: a communications man, a flagman, and an emergency man. Usually there is an assistant flagman and one or more extra emergency men as well. The flagman handles the various flags that transmit information to drivers. The communications man handles the phone or two-way radio that connects his station with other stations and with a central control point at the start/finish line. The emergency men handle fire extinguisher, brooms, wrecking bars, and shovels—all equipment that must be used *away* from the station. Neither flagman nor communications man may leave his post during a race—not even with a four-car wreck smoldering in front of them. Their job is to warn drivers of trouble ahead—not to assist drivers already in trouble—and to keep the chief steward informed of everything that's going on. Only emergency men may leave the station to aid drivers in case of trouble.

The communications man operates the phone at the station—part of the network that extends around the entire course. The network is a "party line"—everyone on it can hear everyone else. To talk himself, the communications man opens his mike by pressing a "talk button." (If all microphones were open all the time, the confusion of track noises would make communication virtually impossible.)

The communications network is a two-way street. Orders go out over it from Control—which flags to display, how to cope with a particular situation, and so on. The flagmen, on the other hand, must relay information back to Control. Unusual conditions must be reported: a car stalled on the track, an accident, oil on the pavement. Frequently the flagman must take the initiative in case of emergency—displaying the caution flag in case of an obstruction on the course, for example. But Control (and hence the chief steward) is always informed instantly.

The flagman's only method of communication with drivers is by means of his flags. There are eight flags (not counting the checkered start/finish flag) and each one speaks clearly to the competition driver. Here's what they say:

GREEN means the course is clear. Drivers may proceed at will.

YELLOW (motionless) means danger. This is the caution flag. It most often means that something—perhaps a spun or stalled car—is partially blocking the track. YELLOW (waved) means that the danger is greater and that drivers must be prepared to stop instantly. Passing is permitted under the yellow flag only when out of the danger area.

RED means STOP! Right now, this instant. And not in the middle of the course, but as much to the edge as possible, so that ambulance or fire truck or wrecker may pass.

WHITE announces that an emergency vehicle is on the course.

The No. 165 Austin-Healey driver was black-flagged on a succeeding lap. His rule infraction: wheels off the course at the start.

YELLOW, VERTICAL RED STRIPES. This flag says, "Take care—there is oil or other slippery substance somewhere on the road."

All of the above five flags apply to all cars on the track. Three additional flags are used to signal a single car, and apply only to the car at which they are directed. These are:

BLACK. "Complete the lap you are now on, then pull into your pit (or other designated location near the start/finish line)." This flag may be used to remove a driver who has committed some rule infraction from a race, or to bring him in to warn him against committing that infraction again. It often acts as a sort of informal disciplinary measure during a race—the time lost during the stop acting as a penalty against the driver. The black flag is also sometimes used to bring in cars, one by one, at the end of a practice or school session.

BLUE WITH YELLOW STRIPE (motionless) tells a driver, "You are being followed very closely."

BLUE WITH YELLOW STRIPE (waved) is more urgent and imperative. It says, "You are blocking a faster car behind you. MOVE OVER!" The blue-and-yellow flag is seldom seen in top-rank racing. Experienced drivers use their mirrors.

BLACK, ORANGE BALL IN CENTER tells a driver that there is something mechanically wrong with his car, orders him to drive carefully to his pit. Frequently cars develop some mechanical trouble that is invisible to the driver—say a dragging tail pipe, a crankcase that is leaking oil, or a bent axle. If the difficulty can be corrected in the pits, the driver may, with official permission, re-enter the race. Otherwise, he's out.

The eight flags are the language of racing. Knowing what they say will make racing a lot more meaningful—and a lot more enjoyable.

Getting A Good View

Just as the enthusiast knows the meaning of the flags, so he also has a pretty good idea of the spots from which he wants to watch the race. Racing isn't like baseball—there's no single spot from which a spectator can see *all* of the "game." So spectators take advantage of the opportunity (afforded them at most courses) of moving from one part of the course to another, picking their own vantage points. Often the entire infield (the area enclosed by the track) is open to spectators, as well as much of the outfield. (See the course maps in Section 3 for the areas open to spectators at each of twenty-one major courses.)

From a spectator's point of view both infield and outfield have their advantages. In the infield it's possible to walk clear to the other side of the course *without* having to walk around it. But the outfield, on the other hand, gives what's often considered to be the best view of the majority of corners—the view from the *outside* of the corner. Many courses have either an underpass or a bridge that permits the spectators to cross from infield to outfield. This prevents the spectator from being irrevocably committed to infield or outfield after the start of a race.

Some courses have grandstands, some have none. But because one can see such a variety of driving by changing position, it seems a shame to stay glued to a few square inches of plank for an entire day's racing. Most people don't tie themselves down this way. Grandstand seats are usually sold at an extra price that's tacked on top of the admission price. Perhaps on an extraordinarily crowded day or at an airport course they're worth it—otherwise not.

Generally speaking, the straightaways are the least exciting spot to watch a race. Here is sheer speed—and little else. But most spectators do enjoy the straights occasionally. Racing straights are just about the only place where you're likely to see cars whipping along at speeds of anywhere from 110 to 160 mph.

Fast bends—turns that are taken at speeds from 75 miles an hour on

Infield spectator area. If one area doesn't suit you, you can always trundle along to the next.

Early morning. Enough spectators do like the grandstands to make choice high seats disappear early.

up—are probably the connisseurs' choice for watching. For it's on the fast turn that the four-wheel drift, the most difficult and dangerous of all driving techniques, can best be seen. Just what drifting is, and how it's done, is explained in Chapter 4.

But down deep, many spectators—the author included—prefer the slower corners. These are the turns that are taken at 70 mph. on down. Some drivers in some cars can still drift through the fastest of these turns. There's more sliding (controlled skidding) in the slow corner. More tight passing maneuvers. More spins. More action in general.

How about the start/finish line? Some like it, some don't. The start is exciting—but it's over in a few seconds. And few races of any distance feature neck-and-neck finishes. Most often the race is decided on the whole length of the track—not in the last few hundred yards. And because starting lines are usually in the middle of straights, there's no cornering to be seen. But being near the starting line has one great advantage. Here the spectator is closest to the pits, the drivers, and everything that's going on, with the exception of the racing itself. You can smell the fuel, hear the engines revving up. The cars are close at hand, which to many people is worth the price of admission in itself. Don't pass up the starting line completely. At a long race—one in which the competitors will make plenty of pit stops—it's particularly exciting.

Chapter 3

STARTS, STRAIGHTS, AND CORNERS

The hands on your watch hit 1:28. The one coming up won't be for practice. An unforgettable smell curls your nose: Castrol mingled with exhaust fumes. One sound carries above crowd noises through the PA system: the rise and fall of the roar from a couple of dozen tail pipes. You look at your program: "F, G, and H Production . . . Race One." They're on the grid now. Looks like this one will get away on time. . . .

Three different kinds of starts are used in American sports car racing: the *Le Mans start,* the *grid start* and the *rolling start.* For pure excitement nothing beats the Le Mans send-off. It takes its name from what's probably the world's greatest sports car race, the twenty-four-hour event at Le Mans, France. In the Le Mans start the cars are parked, engines shut off, along one edge of the track. The drivers line up, opposite their cars, on the other side of the track. At the starter's gun the drivers sprint across the track, clamber into their cars, start their engines, and roar away. It makes for twenty or thirty seconds of pure hysteria at Le Mans— and it's just as pulse-pounding on this side of the Atlantic. Unfortunately from the spectator's point of view, it *isn't* done here very often.

The common American start is the *grid start.* Here the cars are spotted on the track on a painted grid, two or three abreast in alternating rows. Their engines are running. At the start the drivers simply let out their clutches and they're off.

In the grid start the fastest cars are in the front rows. They are picked by their performance in prerace practice or by engine displacement. If all cars have the same engine displacement and no practice

times have been recorded, starting positions are usually determined by lot.

Placing the fastest cars in the front ranks seems as if it gives these cars an unfair advantage. It does. But there's a good reason for it: safety. If the slower cars were forward, they'd be in danger of being overrun by the faster cars, either in the thick of the start or in the scramble on the first turn. This kind of shambles is a smart one to avoid—the unavoidable dangers of racing are great enough. And anyway, a few laps usually manage to even out any unfair handicapping that occurs in the grid start.

The green flag goes down on a grid start.

Sometimes the *rolling start* is used in American sports car racing. In the rolling start, the cars move slowly around the course, led by an official pace car which pulls off the track before arriving at the start/finish line. If all cars are in the proper order as they cross the line, the checkered flag goes down and the cars are off. If the position of the cars is incorrect, a second pace lap is taken until all cars are in proper order as they arrive at the starting line.

Regardless of how the cars are positioned at the start the first turns are likely to be pretty breath-stopping. The press of cars is too thick for anyone to maneuver properly. A spin in the middle of the pack can foul

he Le Mans start in an economy sedan race.

up half a dozen cars and leave them bent and steaming in the middle of the turn. In a longish race expert drivers often hang back to avoid a first turn pile-up—even though it may mean dropping back a number of places. As the classic racing maxim says, "You've got to finish to win."

After a lap or two the cars begin to be more widely spaced around the course. If more than one class of cars is running in the race, now is

The thundering herd crowds through the first turn. A spin here can land a lot of cars in hot water.

the time for the alert spectator to sort out the various classes. Remember that in a multi-class race the over-all leader leads only his class. Some guy half a lap behind him may be leading *his* class and be first in the running for a trophy or a prize that's just as large as the over-all winner's. In a race where the over-all leader is way out front, struggles for position in the other classes (or for second and third in the leader's class) may provide a considerable part of the interest in a race.

Driving on the straightaway requires relatively little technique. Here speed is limited by the top speed of the car's engine and the way in which the car is geared. (See pages 94, 95 for more explanation of gearing.) On some courses the driver must be wary of cross winds (or the lack of them) on long straights at high speed. A gusty cross wind can make frequent corrections in steering necessary. A straight where cross winds may be suddenly blocked by an obstruction (buidings or a trackside grove of trees) must be accorded special care. Many a motorist has noticed this hazard on a highway swept by strong cross winds. Passing a big truck that momentarily blocks the cross wind, he must make instantaneous compensation with the steering wheel to make up for the temporary *lack* of wind.

One interesting piece of technique that may be seen on the straights is "slip-streaming." To slip-stream, a driver tucks his car close in behind a faster car and rides its tail as long as possible. In this position the second car is partially pulled along by the suction and following wind created by the car ahead. The two cars must be very close for the trick to work—say six to fifteen feet! And the second car's potential speed must be close to the lead car's—otherwise the lead car will simply pull away. But if the second car can hang on, he can move considerably faster than he could without the aid of slip-streaming. If his car is superior to the lead car in maneuverability, he may be able to overtake it in a turn. Then, too, there is always the possibility that he may cause the driver of the lead car to bobble—to go too deep into a turn, or overrev his engine in an attempt to escape. His very presence so close behind is likely to be psychologically upsetting to the lead driver. If the lead driver does goof, the slip-streaming driver is in an excellent position to take advantage of the other's mistake. The proximity of the two cars makes slip-streaming a very delicate, very dangerous maneuver. It's for experts only.

Cornering

Where driving skill becomes most evident is in the turns. And it's in *turns* that sports cars and expert sports car drivers are at their remarkable best.

Some turns are gentle enough so that they may be taken flat out—

at full throttle—in high gear. Some, more severe, require a jab at the brake to reduce the car's speed to a rate at which the bend can be safely negotiated. Still others require even harder braking—by means of the car's brakes and *by using the engine as a brake.*

Any car slows when you take your foot off the accelerator. Two things are responsible for this slowing. First, with no power available to overcome internal friction in the engine, this friction acts as a drag on the rear wheels. Second, when your foot is off the accelerator, the pistons meet with greatly increased resistance during one of their four strokes: the intake stroke. Normally these strokes produce only a gentle sucking action through the carburetor. But with your foot off the accelerator, the carburetor is almost completely closed. Now the intake strokes create a strong vacuum in the cylinders, since no air can enter through the carburetor. Pumping this vacuum draws even more power from the rear wheels, and slows the car proportionately.

Engine braking alone will slow a car to a stop. So will use of the brake. *Combining* these two braking forces is the quickest method of slowing the car—and keeping it under control at the same time. But, to get the most out of engine-braking, the engine must be turning over at a relatively high rate of speed (both internal-friction and vacuum-pumping losses increase with engine speed). So in order to keep engine braking at a maximum the car must be shifted down from gear to gear to keep rpm. high as the car slows.

Let's go through a typical down-shift sequence. Imagine yourself in a hypothetical car coming down the straightaway at its maximum speed in top (fourth) gear: 110 mph. Engine speed is at its maximum: 6000 rpm. The turn coming up is a slow one. The car must be dropped to 40 mph. to make it.

When do you start to brake? Only experience can tell you. On an unfamiliar corner you'll go deeper and deeper into the corner on each lap before braking, until you discover the absolute minimum distance necessary for adequate braking. Then you'll mark that point. You may do it mentally—by the "feel" of your distance from the corner. Or you may pick out a marker at the edge of the road—a large stone, a clump of grass, a bush. Some courses have signs that indicate the number of yards to the turn—300, 200, 100. A spot between one of these may be

Not all courses have shut-off points as clearly marked as this one.

the point at which you start to brake. In racing this point is called the "shutoff" or "cutoff" point because it's here that you first shut off or cut off your engine.

At the shutoff point you let up on the accelerator and hit the brake. The combination of engine-braking and your brakes brings your speed down to around 80 . . . and your rpm. down to 4500. Now you make your first down-shift: into third. Engine speed jumps back to 6000 again. Now repeat the process: brake (this time slowing down to about 55 and 4000 rpm., and down-shift into second. Engine speed hits 6000 rpm. again. Now engine-braking, plus a quick application of your brakes, will take you down to the required 40 mph. at which you can make the turn. (If the turn is a very slow one—say, a hairpin that must be crept around at 25 mph.—you would have had to make a third and final down-shift into first gear.) Regardless of the speed of the turn the rule is always "In slow, out fast."

It is obvious that the driver's right foot will be very busy during the down-shift, having to manage both brake and accelerator as it does. (Perhaps the ideal racing driver should be possessed of *two* right feet!)

To overcome the necessity of the right foot having to be in two places at the same time, racing drivers have developed the "heel-and-toe" method of down-shifting. With this method the *toes* of the right foot control the brake while the *heel* controls the accelerator. Or vice versa, depending on the relative location of brake and accelerator pedals in the car. Here's how the heel-and-toe down-shift works:

Step 1: As soon as the driver is ready to slow, his right toes swing off the accelerator and depress the brake. At the same time the heel relaxes pressure on the accelerator, but remains poised over it. Two braking forces are now at work—the engine and the brakes on the car itself.

Step 2: The instant that the car has slowed sufficiently for the next lowest gear to be used, the left foot depresses the clutch pedal and the driver drops from high gear into neutral. His right toes are still on the brake, giving the car as much braking as possible (either a series of jabs or steady pressure on the brake).

Step 3: Now, with the clutch pedal still depressed, the right toes still braking, and the gearshift lever in neutral, the driver's right heel gives the accelerator a quick poke to bring rpm. back up.

Step 4: With clutch still down and rpm. up again, the gearshift lever is dropped into the lower gear. Up comes the clutch pedal and you're ready to start the process all over again if you intend to drop still another gear.

The whole of the heel-and-toe down-shift procedure takes far more time to describe than to accomplish. In the hands of a skilled driver the whole business becomes a series of smoothly synchronized motions that probably take not much more than a second to complete.

The heel-and-toe procedure described above is that used in cars with synchronized gearboxes—which means pretty nearly every modern sports car. But a few cars still have non-synchronized or "crash" gearboxes. And even in cars with synchronized boxes, the synchronization mechanism may be either worn or partially ineffective in fast down-shifting. In such cases the car must be *double-clutched* during the downshift.

As the word "double-clutching" suggests, the clutch must be used *twice* during the down-shift. The extra clutch motion occurs during Step 2 of the heel-and-toe procedure. Here's when, after the gearshift has been moved into neutral, the clutch pedal is let up quickly and then depressed again. During the instant when the pedal is up the driver hits the accelerator with his heel to get the gears spinning at the proper speed for them to engage smoothly. (In the synchronized gearbox a synchronization mechanism gets the gears spinning at the proper speed automatically.) Step 3 is omitted in the double-clutch procedure, and the driver goes directly into Step 4.

Slowed by braking and down-shifting, the car enters the corner. It has reduced its speed enough to make the curve maneuverable, and it is in a gear that will deliver maximum power at that speed. At this point braking ceases. All the work of cornering from here on in is done with steering wheel and accelerator only. Braking in the middle of a turn is a sure invitation to disaster.

The competition driver has at his command three different ways of driving through turns: "going around on rails," sliding, and drifting. Each requires a different proportion of the two major forces that act on a car while it is cornering: forward motion and the centrifugal forces that pull a car sideways in a turn.

"Going around on the rails" is the kind of cornering you do every day on the highway. It is simply cornering at a speed so slow there is no *side* slippage of any wheel. Each wheel moves only in the direction in which it is pointed. It is the slowest and safest method of getting around a corner. It is used in racing only in turns that are so slight they can be mastered at near maximum speeds. On all other turns either the "slide" or the "drift" will be used.

The simplest definition of the slide is simply "controlled wheel skid." Anyone who has done much driving in his or her lifetime has surely experienced a skid. It occurs most commonly when your rear wheels suddenly decide that they will move sideways in addition to forward. It occurs when taking corners too fast on snow or ice or sandy roads, or when you apply the brakes on a curve, or when you accelerate too hard in a curve. Suddenly you feel your rear wheels sliding outward in a most disconcerting way. A quick motion of the steering wheel or a lessening of pressure on the accelerator or brake corrects it.

But this very same kind of skidding, so unpleasant on the road, is put to good use by the racing driver. On the race course, however, it is induced by use of the accelerator pedal, not by the brake. In the turn

the driver simply applies enough power to the rear wheels to break
some of their traction on the road. When this occurs, the rear wheels
tend to slide toward the outside of the curve, as well as to roll forward
along the road. The car points itself more in the direction of the curve,
and as this occurs, the front wheels are straightened out to take advantage of the car's new position. (If the front wheels are not straightened,

The drift—a precarious balance of forward motion with sideways sliding.

the result will be a spin to the inside edge of the track.) The slide may
be executed either as one long continuous sweep (rear wheels constantly
sliding outward, front wheels cocked in such a manner as to prevent
spinning) or as a series of little slides joined with steering corrections in
the front wheels. Either way the slide requires delicate handling of
both accelerator and steering to prevent spinning.

The *drift* is the most difficult technique of cornering—and consistently
good drifting is the mark of the expert competition driver. In the simplest terms it is a *four-wheel slide* in which all of the car's wheels are

*A slide—uncontrolled—quickly becomes a
spin-out. Watch No. 244. His rear end
breaks away . . . he skids off the course
backwards . . . he makes a quick check for
damage to the car . . . no damage done,
he prepares to re-enter.*

slipping sideways as well as rolling forward. It is a high-speed technique
. . . some slower cars will not drift no matter how expert their drivers.

Basically the drift consists of cornering with all four wheels lined up
—the front wheels pointed straight ahead. How can the car turn? By
a delicate balancing of the two forces that act upon it in a corner—
forward momentum against sideways slip. The first pulls the car ahead
in a straight line; the second pulls it in a direction at right angles to
that straight line. So that in the drift the car is moving forward and
sideways *at the same time.* It is a technique so delicate that even the best
drivers find it hard to describe. Ideally it is one smooth sweep. In practice, however, it is usually a series of tiny corrections: a bit of accelerator to position the rear wheels, the lightest twitch of the steering wheel
to position the front ones. The crucial thing, however, is to keep all
four wheels sliding as well as rolling.

Racing drivers speak of the proper "line" through a bend or corner.
"Line" is simply the path the car follows . . . and the best one is that
which enables the car to get around the turn in the least possible time
(or sometimes, when a second corner closely follows the first) in the
best possible position for the next corner. Remember that the racing
driver can use *both* sides of the road on a sports car course. The expert
uses every inch of it . . . from the extreme right hand edge to the
extreme left-hand edge. By so doing he can make a sharp turn considerably less sharp than it would be if he were forced to remain on the
right hand side of the road.

Where the corner is both preceded and followed by some amount of
straight road, the proper line is one that finds the car at the far *outside*
of the road before the curve, at its absolute *inside* edge at the apex of
the turn, and again at the *outside* of the road at the exit from the curve.
This is known as "using all the road." Sometimes such a line is impossible. If the road has an abnormal slant or camber to it, for example.
Or if the turn is one of a series of closely linked curves—left-handers
and right-handers following closely one under the other. (Such sequences
are frequently referred to as "esses.") The proper line through a series
of turns is that which gives the quickest over-all time through the series.
Frequently this means abandoning the best line for one of the turns
in order to be better positioned for the others.

Nine cars using every inch of the road in a beautiful demonstration of "line."

A driver's *over-all* time around a circuit is of course the true measure of his (and his car's) performance. *Lap time*—the time it takes to cover one lap around the course—is a figure of vital concern to both the driver and his pit crew. Lap times are inversely proportional to miles per hour. But since the former can be read directly from a stop watch, driver's speeds are usually discussed in terms of time rather than mph. "He lapped Watkins Glen in 1:25," or "The lap record at Continental Divide is 1:95" are simple examples. Many racing spectators carry stop watches so that they can check lap times for themselves. Many of the programs at races carry tables for converting lap times into mph. for those who are interested.

Seconds add up fast in sports car racing. At an average speed of 80 mph. a car that's only one second per lap faster than the competition will be over half a mile ahead of that competition at the end of a twenty-five-lap race! On each lap the faster car lengthens the distance between himself and the following cars by almost forty yards—eight or more car lengths. One of the pit crew's important jobs during a race is keeping its driver posted on his lap times and position via blackboards or other signs. This job is most important during long races, when pit stops and overtakings may have made position and relative speed almost a complete mystery to the driver.

Up to the present time long races have been the exception rather than the rule in American sports car racing. This is largely a result of the overwhelmingly amateur nature of the sport in this country. With the majority of amateurs neither their cars, nor their pit crews, nor their pocketbooks are equal to the demands of a six-hour or a five-hundred-mile race. Thus at least nine out of ten races in this country are less than seventy-five miles or one hour long. But some of the most interesting and best-known American races are comparatively long-distance races . . . like the twelve-hour classic at Sebring or the annual five-hundred-mile Road America event at Elkhart Lake, Wisconsin.

Strategy and Tactics

The difference between "strategy" and "tactics" is generally considered to be that between over-all planning of a battle or event and the minute-by-minute action that must be taken as special circumstances arise. In short sports car races there's a minimum of strategy involved. Tactics—when to pass, how fast to corner, etc.—are generally on-the-spot decisions made by the driver. The only strategy consists of driving just fast enough to come in first. When the competitive situation makes demands on the driver in a short race, he can usually meet them without giving thought to an over-all plan. In short races there's less need for a driver to spare his engine (or his brakes)—since both engines and brakes can be overworked for relatively brief periods of time. No need to think about sparing tires—for even the fastest, roughest driver finds it hard to wear out a brand-new set of racing tires in most fifty-mile races. No need to worry about fuel stops—a tankful is always good for fifty miles. The planning of pit stops in general is unnecessary—any difficulty serious enough to require more than a thirty-second pit stop is serious enough to lose a short race. (Even in short races, however, competitors do on occasion run out of gas! When this happens, it means that the driver has cut too fine a line between carrying enough fuel and keeping his car light. *Not* carrying unnecessary gas is standard racing practice. Why burden your car with extra gallons—six pounds each—if you're not going to need them?)

Long-distance racing—say of two hundred fifty miles and up—is a different story. Here good strategy is almost as important as good tactics and skilled driving. Winning strategy in a long race means that someone has to come up with the right answers to questions like these:

Should the car be driven a bit slower to try to last the whole race on one set of tires? Or should it be pushed faster at the risk of a time-consuming pit stop for changing wheels?

Should the race be run on several partial fuel fill-ups, hoping that lightness and maybe better weight distribution will make up for an extra stop?

How soon should the first pit stop be made? In the case of team cars how should fuel be apportioned so that not all cars are in the team pits at one time?

Should the car be headed for the lead and kept there, sparing it and its drivers the difficult job of trying to pass a determined front-runner? Or should it be held back, in the hope that the strain of holding the lead will damage the leading car, or tempt its driver into trying to take a corner too fast?

How will driving duties (if two drivers are to handle the car) be split up? Which driver will be faster after dark? In the rain? And what are the chances of rain?

There are many other strategic posers, most if not all of them just as tough. In the case of an individual car, owner and driver or owner/ driver will decide them, perhaps with the advice of members of the pit crew. In the case of a factory team, or a team entered by a dealer or private owner, generally a team manager—usually *not* a driver—will decide the strategy. Much of it will be decided before the race. But some decisions will depend on unforeseen events: mechanical difficulties, weather conditions, and the like. One thing is certain—in a long race good planning (including planning for the unexpected) is of crucial importance.

Which is more important in winning sports car races: good drivers or good cars? It is difficult to say. Surely a good driver can perform wonders even in a mediocre machine. But in few other sports is good equip-

"You've got to finish to win." This Lister-Jaguar did both. "Passenger" is team manager, very appropriately sharing the congratulations.

ment so vital to success. True, in sailing or polo a good boat or a fine stable is a "must." But a good bat never made a batting champion, nor specially modified sneakers a high point-scorer on the basketball court.

If winning equipment were available to all drivers, sports car racing would be more truly competitive than it is. But the owner of a really good piece of machinery—particularly good modified machinery— is naturally anxious to see it well driven. Unless the owner is himself a fine driver, it is likely that sooner or later he will get a good driver to drive it for him. So good cars tend to find their way into the hands of top drivers. Which makes it tough on the little guy—the guy who cannot afford top tuning, frequent rebuilds, or perhaps even an expensive car in the first place. This is nothing the sport need apologize for. Certainly it is under no obligation to "give the little guy a chance." But without detracting a whit from the accomplishments of drivers who are consistent winners, it seems clear that they owe something to the superiority of their mounts. Most of them would be among the first to agree.

It is worth remembering that the successful competition driver is successful in *two* kinds of competition. One is the more obvious kind—the competition with other drivers. The second is less obvious but in some ways more dramatic. This is the kind of competition in which the driver competes with himself. For he must have the guts to put his car and his personal safety "on the ragged edge" time after time after time. Only the driver who can come close to this edge, perilously close, can be a true champion. In this kind of competition motor racing closely parallels the bullfight. Whether a man can kill a bull is unimportant. What *is* important is how close he dares come to the horns.

Chapter 4

GETTING BEHIND THE WHEEL

You stay at the fence long enough to watch the big red Ferrari roll by one more time. It's alone now . . . and not screaming by as it did during the race. But the checkered flag held by the girl in the passenger seat snaps proudly. Victory lap must be quite a thrill. Too bad the Corvette special didn't hold together . . . it looked pretty good for the first few laps. That expensive Italian machinery is hard to beat. You turn and amble back toward the parking lot. Like to go racing myself, you think.

The first thing anyone needs to get started in sports car racing is *plenty of driving experience.* Thousands of miles on turnpikes and dirt roads, in summer and in winter, on dry roads and icy ones. They needn't all be in a sports car . . . pushing a '52 Ford or a Hillman Minx can turn up plenty of valuable experience in control, cornering, braking, and the like. Many of the small imported sedans—the Volkswagen, Fiat 600 Renault R-8, for example—offer much that is sports-car-like in gearing and handling, if not in performance.

Sooner or later a real sports car will enter the picture. More than likely it'll be one of the less expensive English ones: a Sprite or an MG, perhaps. As a choice made with an eye toward eventually racing, either of these would be excellent. Their low cost will keep a bunged-up fender or a bent valve from being a major economic disaster. They're easy to work on, if you want to do it yourself . . . and cheaper to repair if you have to have someone else do it. There's plenty of good competition to be found for them—something that can't be said of all makes. Moreover, since they are popular "beginner's" cars, there's plenty of less-than-expert competition to be found. No fledgling driver should reasonably want to start off competing against too many experts. Lastly, neither of these cars is too much of a handful for the beginning sports car driver. The MG, in particular, is fast and powerful enough to suit most beginners' skills and tastes, yet has a reputation as being a marvelously "forgiving" car—it will withstand a lot of bad driving *without* ending up upside down or against a tree.

Ready for racing? Not by a long shot. Experience in *sports cars*—the more the better—is essential. Here's where it can be gotten:

Back-Roads Driving

Since the essence of racing is cornering, better get in as much mileage as possible in corners. The average turnpike or highway is much too straight to give you anything but a lazy top-gear spin. But back-country black top is another story. This kind of road is what the road-racing circuit is designed to duplicate. All the trials of cornering, bumpy surfaces, bad camber, uphill and downhill acceleration can be found on hundreds of thousands of miles of American back road. None of us, no matter how city-bound, live more than an hour or two's drive from this kind of road. On it you can put in hour after hour of practice in down-shifting, heel-and-towing, braking, cornering, and digging out.

Caution: *No all-out high speed driving on back roads!* First of all, it's illegal. Secondly, it's downright dangerous. And though the dangers are obvious, they're worth pointing out just in case you're tempted. *Two-way traffic.* Even the most deserted country curve may have a '38 Plymouth bumbling around it in the other direction. *Roadside hazards.* Slide off the road at most sports car courses and you bump a haybale, plow some sand, scrape a fence, or chew up some turf. Not so on the road, where a solid oak, a stone wall or a thirty-foot drop-off is likely to be your fate. *Unexpected hazards.* Unforeseen dangers like the turn that suddenly gets tighter. Wet leaves that suddenly appear under your wheels. A pothole that can toss you off the road if you hit it wrong. A prime requisite for racing is *knowing the course*—and on public roads you never do. All-out efforts should be saved for the course.

Rallies

Unlike European rallies, which often are run at near-racing speeds, in part on racing circuits, the American rally offers little that is directly useful in racing. Yet the rally does present a chance to gain useful all-around driving experience and play a challenging game while doing so.

The American rally is a kind of motorized hare-and-hounds game, requiring the entrants to follow a more or less complicated route at precise speeds. As they say, a rally is *not* a race. Rallies are planned so that, ideally, no speed in excess of legal speed will be required. Frequently contestants are more heavily penalized for driving *over* required speeds than for driving below them—to discourage speeding. The great majority of rallies in this country are completed in less than a day, and many are simply a Saturday- or Sunday-afternoon tour of a hundred or so miles. A few rallies are two- or three-day events—the championship rallies run by the SCCA are typical. Besides your car, an inexpensive timer (stop watch or the like), a book of average speed tables or a circular slide rule, a clip board and pencil and paper are all that are really necessary to compete in a rally, though some rallyists spend hundreds of dollars on fancy timers and computers. You'll need a navigator to follow direction sheets and make calculations, since you'll be doing the driving yourself. You can find nearby rallies scheduled in the sports car columns of local newspapers or, if you're a sports car club member, through your club.

Gymkhanas

The gymkhana is the tamest of all speed events, yet one that offers valuable experience to the would-be racing driver. A gymkhana is usually made up of several events held on a parking lot, large or small. One of the events is sure to be a trial something like the slalom in skiing. A tight, twisty course is marked out by pylons or other marking devices. Competing cars drive through it, one at a time. The object is to complete the course as quickly as possible without knocking over any of the markers. It is, in effect, a tiny, low-speed sports car race—except for the fact that only one car is on the course at one time. Another event may be a "parking test," in which the car is timed in getting in and out of a tiny parking space. Another may be a balloon-spearing contest, for which a co-driver is required. Or a braking test in which you wind up to 30 mph. and then must stop with your front wheels exactly on a given line. Ingenuity and space are the only limits to the organizer of a gymkhana. A gymkhana gives you good experience at handling your car accurately and fast, while keeping your speed way down. Because of the low speeds involved generally no more safety equipment than a seat belt is required, and in some gymkhanas even that may be waived. Low speeds are of course pretty good insurance against doing any damage to your car.

Ice Races

Ice races offer a chance for real, honest-to-goodness sports car racing . . . with the risk of doing damage to anything but your car's bodywork pretty well taken out of it. Ice races are held on frozen lakes, on a course marked by pylons or hay bales. The length of the course depends on the size of the lake, but anything from half a mile to two miles is common. The beauty of the ice race is that it exaggerates to an extreme degree the common racing problems of traction, cornering, and acceleration. Yet the slipperiness of the surface keeps speeds low.

Ice races are generally brief in duration (perhaps enough laps to add up to ten or twenty miles). Cars run in displacement classifications, just as they do in sports car road racing. (The size and power of the car are far less crucial in ice-racing, however, since the lack of traction can whittle Corvettes right down to Volkswagen size.) The most successful cars in ice-racing are those with a large proportion of their weight over their driving wheels—Porsches, MG Sports Sedans. The otherwise-unwarlike Saab sedan—front-wheel drive and designed for icy Scandinavian roads—is a real terror in ice racing.

The surface encountered in ice-racing is not always ice. Frequently it is hard-packed snow that has accumulated on the ice. But either way it is slippery enough to induce extreme sliding and uncontrollable spinning if you ask too much of it. So there's an awfully good chance of banging up your car by spinning or sliding into the way of another. If you're not prepared to take that chance, stay off the ice. Ice, on the other hand, is almost impossible to roll on—you skid or spin rather than flip over.

Preparing a car for ice-racing is simple. It usually consists of no more than lowering the pressure in tires (for better traction), shifting what weight you can over the driving wheels, and taping your headlights. Chains and snow tires are almost always barred. Generally speaking, some safety equipment *is* required—helmet, safety belt, and possibly a fire extinguisher. Roll bars are seldom in order, because of extreme unlikelihood of rolling. Generally, a competition license is not required. If you don't mind risking your paint and fenders, ice-racing is a barrel of fun—all the stresses and excitement of competition driving, with practically none of the danger.

Hill Climbs

Closest to road-racing in both danger and difficulty, the hill climb is still less demanding than road-racing. Two factors contribute to this. First, hill-climbing is inevitably slower than course-racing, because the slope of the hill effectively slows the car. Second, each car runs alone on the hill, removing the possibility of collision with other cars. A typical hill climb will be over a road anywhere from one to three miles long, winding steeply up a hill or mountain. Cars run against the clock, one at a time, and not against each other. If time and the number of entries permit, a driver will be given several runs. Usually the best of his runs will be scored.

Hill-climb speeds are high enough, and hill-climb courses difficult enough, to make full safety equipment generally required at such events. Helmets, safety belts, and fire extinguishers are usually mandatory, as are roll bars in the case of open cars. While some smaller local hill climbs may ignore the desirability of roll bars, it is dangerous to compete without one. Both organizers and competitors run a considerable risk if roll bars are not mandatory.

Several hill-climb courses have long and exciting histories, and are apt to attract top drivers and cars. Mount Equinox, in southern Vermont, and Giant's Despair Mountain, near Wilkes-Barre, Pennsylvania, are the scenes of two annual major hill climbs. Many small clubs sponsor hill climbs on local hills, and any one of these events will make an exciting day's sport for the sports car owner. (Many of these smaller events do not require competition licenses, by the way.) The competition among production cars is likely to be hot. Good driving—particularly good cornering and careful acceleration on surfaces that frequently will not provide traction for full power—pays off here.

On to Racing

Okay . . . suppose you've had your fill of minor-league events and are ready to really go sports car racing. Not on a parking lot, frozen lake, or mountainside, but on real, live road course. How do you go about it?

First step (if you haven't already taken it) is to join a sports car club that runs driver's schools, issues competition licenses, and sponsors races. The best choice is the SCCA, whose competition setup for amateurs is the only one which covers the entire country. Virtually all important American amateur racing is conducted under the SCCA's aegis. A number of smaller clubs also sponsor races and issue competition licenses. But if racing's your aim, make sure the club you choose *races*. (Many are involved only in rallying, gymkhanas, socializing, etc.)

Odds are that it'll be the SCCA you join. Their national headquarters in Westport, Connecticut, will put you in touch with the SCCA region (the sixty-odd local units of the SCCA are called "regions") in your area. From the region you get an application blank. This is returned to the region with $13.50 ($10 national dues and $3.50 for a subscription to the club magazine, *Sports Car*) plus whatever dues the region may require. In addition, you need letters of recommendation from two SCCA members, and a letter of your own describing your interests and reasons for wishing to join the club. Once you're an SCCA (or other racing club) member, you're ready to go after a competition license.

If you don't already own one, you'll need a helmet. Make sure the one you buy is one of the models approved by your club for racing. Regardless of the question of approval don't try to scrimp here. Your life may depend on it. Recently a great deal of outstanding research and testing have been done on helmets by the Snell Foundation, a non-profit organization set up in memory of a West Coast driver who was killed by head injuries incurred in a crash. As a result of Snell Foundation work much has been done to improve helmets. Good helmets cost around $40, and are well worth it. The Bell and Buco racing helmets are two of the best-known. Get the opinions of some owners before you buy. Shatterproof goggles or face shield will complete your headgear.

Chances are that you'll also need flame-resistant coveralls or other garments. These should be long-sleeved, to cover your wrists, and have some provision for keeping trouser cuffs from flapping loose around the ankles. Most coveralls can be made flame-resistant by dipping in various commercial flame retardants. Or the job can be done with ten ounces of borax and eight ounces of boric acid dissolved in a gallon of hot water. Garments must be dipped in this solution at least three times and dried between dippings. The treatment must be repeated each time the garments are washed or dry-cleaned.

For your car you *must* have three competition accessories: seat belts, a fire extinguisher, and a roll bar. If you haven't got seat belts installed already, shame on you! Every bit of evidence shows that they reduce injuries greatly in serious accidents, save lives frequently, and often prevent injuries completely in minor accidents. It is true that some top European drivers dislike wearing them. It is possible, however, that at the extremely high speeds of 140 mph. and up, encountered by these drivers, being thrown out of the car may offer more hope of survival, particularly when the car is a lightweight modified machine incapable of absorbing much energy. Certainly there have been a few almost miraculous instances of drivers being thrown from cars and surviving in recent European racing history. The safety belt is widely accepted as a life- and injury-saving device, however. It may be that the club you join sets minimum standards for safety belts. Check with them before buying; it's better than not being allowed to get on the course because a belt doesn't measure up. While fitting out your car with a belt, make it *two*—one for the passenger's side as well. Proper installation of the belt is extremely important, by the way. It should be anchored to the *frame* of the car if possible, and if not, anchored in such a way that it won't pull loose the first time severe pressure is put against it.

Safety equipment: approved helmet, face shield, fireproof clothing. Padded head rest conceals roll bar, safety belt is hidden in driver's lap.

Your club will also be likely to have set up minimum requirements for fire extinguishers. The SCCA says that extinguishers must be at least one pound if carbon dioxide, two pounds if dry chemical. Carbon tetrachloride extinguishers are not allowed. The extinguisher should be securely mounted—in the cockpit and close at hand. Chances are that the driver will be the man nearest his car if a fire breaks out, and other fire extinguishers on the course may be either out of reach or already in use. An extinguisher in the luggage compartment (perhaps in a luggage compartment that's jammed shut) is of little use.

The major item that must be installed is a roll bar. Even if regulations didn't call for one, you'd be a fool to race without it. For a number of years many "pros" scoffed at them. Today they are almost universally required—and almost universally blessed. Most cars will permit the installation of roll bars without any cutting of the body material. If you plan to use your car for both racing and touring, plan to get a roll bar that can be removed when not needed for racing safety. Excellent and good-looking roll bars are now available commercially, and there are plenty of sports car garages around that can turn out hand-made ones.

Now you're ready to race . . . and your car's ready to race. Except for one thing: a competition license. Just joining a club isn't enough to let you out on the race course; you've got to have proof that you're capable of driving in competition. That proof is a competition license, issued by the club. To get one, you'll probably have to go to *driver's school.* You will have to attend one or more, until the instructors feel that you're ready to be awarded a competition license. (You may at first be issued some sort of temporary competition license, to be exchanged for a full-fledged license after you've competed without incident in a specified number of races.)

The typical driver's school is a weekend affair held on a nearby racing circuit. It starts with a rigorous safety inspection of your car and equipment. Tires will be checked for tread and condition. There's a brake test; you run your car up to around 20 mph., take your hands off the wheel, and jam on your brakes. Any sign of "pulling" (veering to the left or right) with your hands off the wheel calls for brake adjustment before you're allowed on the course. Wheel bearings, exhaust system,

Technical inspection...a complete pre-race safety check.

cooling system, suspension and steering, shock absorbers, stop light, safety belt, roll bar, fire extinguisher—all will be checked. (This inspection duplicates the one that cars are given before entering most races.)

Next on the agenda comes some observing of experienced drivers running on the course. Accompanied by instructors (usually old racing hands), the class goes out on the course. *On foot.* You gather around Turn One, if it's an interesting one, and watch as half a dozen experienced

drivers push their cars through the turn. The instructors point out
what's going on—the shutoff, the down-shift, the entrance, the slide or
drift, the line, the exit—and comment on the right and wrong ways to
take the turn. Then it's on to Turn Two, where the same process is repeated. You can spend a good half day this way—walking, watching,
walking, watching. Incidentally, it's not uncommon for the most experienced drivers to walk an unfamiliar course to check surfaces, shoulders,
and the like before racing on it. So a turn around it on foot is anything
but silly stuff.

*A group of fledgling drivers stop, look, and learn about cornering. This is
driver's school. Their next step is do-it-yourself.*

Finally, it'll be time to do some driving. First a few laps under the
yellow (caution, no passing) flag, just to get the feel of the course. Then,
if everything seems to be going smoothly, the green flag will go out, and
you'll be able to give it everything you've got. But despite the green
flag this is *not* a race. It's a test of your driving know-how: your line
through corners, your acceleration out of them, your passing technique,

and all the rest. It'll do you no good to pass every car on the course, if you insist on sliding off the course at that slow turn at the end of the straight. Every move you make will be noted by observers spotted along the course. Keep muffing that slow corner, and you'll hear about it when the practice session is over. If you find you're having problems you can't solve yourself, usually you can pull in at the start/finish and ask one of the instructors to go around with you, correcting your mistakes. Don't let pride keep you from asking—it's less embarrassing than being black-flagged and *ordered* to take a tour with an instructor.

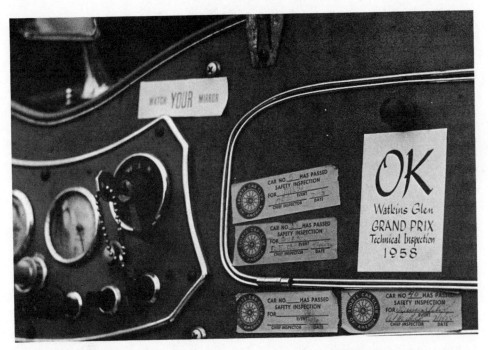

Five safety inspection stickers, five race meets. And as this MG's owner would probably testify, five pretty expensive weekends.

How soon you get your competition license is entirely up to you. It's likely to take several driver's schools, however, unless you're either unusually expert or an unusually quick learner.

More than likely your first races after you get your license will be either small, local events or novice races. While you may be itching to get into the "big time," remember that the experience you get in novice

Last-minute adjustments keep driver and pit crew member busy.

events is every bit as valuable. Moreover, you'll have a much better
chance of performing well in novice events *without* spending a potful of
money on the tuning, modifications, and tires you'll need to do well in
the big events.

For racing *is* expensive. Not if you're good enough to be asked to drive
a car owned and maintained by someone else, of course. But there's
little likelihood of that happening early in your career. Chances are
that you'll be footing your own bills for quite a while. And they do
mount up.

First off, you've got to figure on traveling and living expenses for the
weekend. Few drivers are lucky enough to live next door to a course.
If a wife comes with you, somebody may have to stay with the kids at
home.

Pit crew member on a racing team has three cars to keep informed. (Problem: why is car 59 lapping two seconds slower than the other two team cars?)

If you're planning to do any serious racing—even in the production classes—it's likely to cost you several hundred dollars to get your car in racing trim in the first place. While balancing, port-matching, and polishing (see Chapter 5) aren't absolutely indispensable, it's certain that *winning* cars will have had these operations performed. Your car is likely to need frequent tuning, and equally frequent replacement of parts worn or weakened by racing stresses. If you can do these jobs yourself, fine. If you can't, they'll cost you. One thing you'll need plenty of is *tires,* because nothing chews 'em up faster than racing. They cost, too— particularly the fancier racing varieties. If entrance fees are required, they too will have to be counted in. All in all, you can figure on a racing weekend costing you several hundred dollars. If you're racing to *win,* that is.

If your budget can't stand this kind of a bite, there are other ways to get involved in racing that cause practically no pain in the pocketbook. One way is to go as a race worker—to do a job in communications, flagging or timing. Members of sports car clubs that sponsor races will find themselves in constant demand as race personnel if they are properly trained. Training with the larger clubs may actually involve a weekend communications school where flagging and communications procedures are taught. Or, particularly in the case of smaller clubs and events, it may consist of a five-minute briefing before the races. Working at a race is one of the best ways to see racing—close up—at no cost other than transportation and baby-sitters.

Or you may be lucky enough to join a driver's pit crew and help with the preparation of the car, refueling, and the like. If you're a reasonably good mechanic, drivers are likely to seek *you* out. If not, there are tasks that will keep even the mechanical numskull busy—timing laps, signaling, and the like. Most entrants in amateur events are given a certain number of "pit passes" to accommodate a limited number of the helping hands they may wish to bring along. Of course you'll be expected to work, not loaf, if you come as part of a driver's crew.

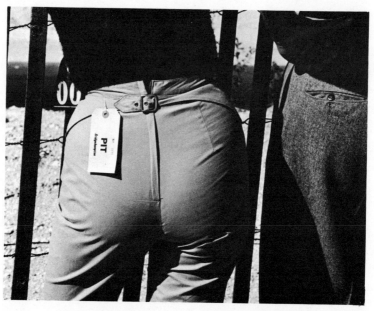

They also serve who stand and decorate.

THE CARS

What makes the modern sports car?

It cannot be simply engine design. For among the cars described in the following pages are to be found engines with four, six, eight, and twelve cylinders, V-engines, in-line engines and flat engines, engines with two, three, and four carburetors (and several with fuel injection), engines with one camshaft, two camshafts . . . even as many as four camshafts.

Is it brakes, then? Hardly, when inboard and outboard, drum and disc all are represented.

Body material? No . . . some are of steel, some of aluminum, some of fiberglass.

Rear-end design? Not that, either. Take your pick among "live" rear axles, de Dion suspensions, and fully independent rear ends.

But why go on? Clearly, it is not any specific set of design features that makes a sports car.

Nor is it looks or visual "sportiness" that makes a sports car. Take the two-seat Thunderbird or the Volkswagen Karmann-Ghia convertible. What could *look* more like a sports car? Yet neither of these two beauties is worth a hoot on the race course.

Let us be clear about it. The sports car cannot be judged by what it *is*. It can only be judged by what it *does*. And what it does—what all do well, and the great ones do magnificently—is *perform well on the road*. And on the road *means* on the road. Any road . . . winding or straight, rough or smooth, banked or flat, narrow or wide.

Plenty of acceleration? Sure. An impressive top speed? That too. Nimble steering . . . quick, no-fade braking . . . sure, agile cornering . . . remarkable durability under stress? Add these in, too. There isn't a one of them you can do without—unless you're willing to sacrifice some of that good performance on the road.

What all this adds up to in sports car design is this: the car must be a *balanced* car. A car in which no one part is significantly weaker than its fellows. The car should possess all of its attributes in equal quantities—its engine should not be too much for its brakes, its body and frame should not be too heavy for its engine, nor its brakes too large for its wheels.

So the sports car designer must be a man of infinite compromise. Because as in all design, few features can be improved except at the expense of other features. Take even so simple an object as a coffee cup. It's no trick at all to design a cup that's absolutely unbreakable and unstainable. You use stainless steel. Which does indeed make an unstainable, unbreakable cup . . . but one that is too costly, too heavy, and burns the skin off the first fingers that touch it! Or try making a pencil that gives you a beautiful black line without the drawback of frequent sharpenings. You can sharpen seldom only if you're willing to settle for a hard gray point. And what is true in the design of lead pencils and coffee cups is multiplied a thousandfold in the case of the sports car.

Take the age old question of lightness *vs.* strength. A car frame that is indescribably strong can be built . . . if a half ton of steel can be used to do it. But the sports car must be light to be fast.

Or power *vs.* reliability. There is practically no sports car engine in existence today whose power could not be significantly increased . . . if the car is only to lead the pack for one fast lap and then sit out the rest of the race as a blown-apart junk heap of pistons, rods, and valves. Few steady racegoers have missed the demise of one or more home-built "specials" whose builders have tried to squeeze a few more horses from their already-overstressed engines.

Balance. That's what a sports car must have. Balance between top speed and acceleration . . . light weight and sturdiness . . . power and reliability . . . and many other factors, all mutually opposed.

In the evolution of the sports car there is practically no design feature that has not been tried. And by going through a natural process of selection and rejection some features have proved themselves most suitable for good road performance. (Not all of these are feasible in the mass-produced sports car, simply because they are too expensive.) But it is pretty sure that a car that embodies *none* of them will be neither successful nor popular.

Engines

One of the first questions the sports car designer must decide about the engine starts not with "what" or "which," but "where." *Where* should the engine be located—front or rear?

While a number of considerations affect engine location, the most important is undoubtedly that of *weight distribution.* For many years, it was believed that for perfect handling, the weight on the rear wheels of the car should be close to that on the front wheels . . . giving what is referred to as 50/50 weight distribution. This belief conflicted with a simple fact: that for maximum traction, the more weight on the driving (rear) wheels, the better. Fortunately, modern suspension design has been able to reconcile this conflict remarkably well. Most of the really successful big-engined machinery today is rear-engined. Cars with as much as 60 or 65 per cent of their weight on the rear wheels can be made to handle as well or better than those with more equal weight distribution. One remarkably successful car—the Porsche—has been rear-engined for almost two decades.

There are other advantages to a rear-engined racer. Rear-engine design does away with a heavy drive shaft that runs from a front-mounted engine to the rear of the car. And you can build your transmission and differential all in one unit—for convenience, simplicity, and lowered weight.

Then why aren't *all* engines rear-mounted? Cost, for one thing. Many small sports cars can be sold at a competitive price only because of their extensive use of parts from passenger cars. Most passenger cars are still front-engined. A second cost factor: the rear-mounted engine requires an expensive kind of rear suspension—fully-independent rear suspension.

Cooling is another factor: if you need a big radiator for water-cooling, it works more easily up front, where the air stream is. But this means water lines must run from the front of the car all the way back to the rear-mounted engine. For the mass-produced sports car, this is both too complex and too expensive. For the specially built sports racer, of course, it is no problem. The Lola 70, the Lotus 30, the Ford GT, and the rear-engined Ferrari sports and GT cars all have front-mounted radiators. Porsche, of course, continues to simplify matters by sticking to air-cooling.

Strictly speaking, many of the cars referred to as rear-engined are not that. To the purist, a rear-engined car has its engine *behind* transmission and differential. Rear engines located ahead of the transmission (as are most today) are located "midship."

Whatever its location, the good sports car engine should be powerful, durable, and light. There is no magic number of cylinders that yields a perfect balance of all three. Current practice generally calls for four cylinders in smaller engines—up to 1600 cc. Four-cylinder engines are of course cheaper to produce than those with more cylinders—important in keeping cost down. But the four is fine for racing, too. It's simple, first and foremost. Two dual-throat carburetors (more about those in a minute) can efficiently supply it with all the fuel it can ever consume. Engines with more than four cylinders require either more carburetors or more complicated carburetors to make them perform at maximum efficiency. The four-cylinder engine is short and compact. Its crankshaft, being short, can be sturdy without unnecessary weight. It requires fewer bearings—and every bearing in an engine is a potential trouble spot. Four-cylinder engines are generally in-line engines, the cylinders perpendicular to the ground and lined up one behind the other. However, in the Porsche the arrangement of the four cylinders is opposed. The Porsche engine is like two little two-cylinder in-line engines, each laid on its side so that its cylinders are parallel to the ground. The pairs of cylinders are opposite each other on a horizontal plane, so the engine is said to be opposed. The more conventional four-cylinder in-line engine is to be found in the MG, the Alfa, and the Sprite. The famous 1100 cc. Coventry Climax engine (still used in some smaller Lotuses, Lolas, and Elvas) is also an in-line four. The Porsche 904 has a flat four, but the Porsche 911 engine is a flat six. Ferrari has built both 4-cylinder 2-liter engines and V-6's.

Above two liters, six or more cylinders definitely take over. The most-favored designs are the V-8 (Corvette and Ford Cobra), the V-12 (Ferrari is the leading exponent of this design), and the in-line six (Jaguar, Aston Martin). While V-engines can be built shorter and lower than in-line engines, they require twice as many camshafts if the designer wishes to use a double overhead camshaft design. Expense and complexity are naturally increased. But big overhead valve V-8's like the Chevrolet, Ford, and Olds can develop race-adequate horsepower without overhead camshafts—by virtue of sheer size, aided by careful tuning and modification.

Virtually all sports car engines (with the exception of the no-valve two-cycle jobs) have overhead valves. The location of the camshaft, by which the valves are opened and closed, however, varies considerably with the price and efficiency of the engine. Generally speaking, the least expensive and least efficient location for the camshaft is in the engine block. When it is located there, an extra set of moving parts called push rods transmits the motion of the cams up through the head of the engine to rocker arms that actuate the valves. The MG, Austin-Healey, Triumph, Volvo, Porsche 912, and a number of other production engines all employ push-rod overhead valves.

A greatly superior location for the camshaft is atop the cylinder head itself. Almost all truly high-performance engines use this location. Here the camshaft can act directly on all the valves (if the valves are in line). If the valves are not in line, the camshaft may actuate half the valves directly and the other half indirectly via an arrangement of pivoted fingers. Or the camshaft may actuate both sets of valves by these fingers. (Remember that a V-engine of single-overhead-cam design requires *two* cams, one for each bank of cylinders.) Engines employing the single overhead cam include the Coventry Climax 1100 cc., the Mercedes-Benz 300SL, and the Porsche 911.

The ultimate refinement in valve actuation is the double overhead camshaft. With double overhead camshafts each row of valves can be operated directly by its own camshaft, even when the rows are inclined at different angles (as they should be for best combustion-chamber design). Engines that employ double overhead camshafts include the Jaguar, the Alfa Romeo, the Porsche Carrera and 904 engines, and the Ferrari 250LM, 275P, and 330P. Double-overhead camshafts are the mark of the high-efficiency racing engine.

It is interesting to note that a number of engines have had their power significantly increased by the installation of double overhead camshafts as a major modification. Abarth's most potent Fiat transformations use double-overhead camshafts. And it's a Lotus twin-cam version of an English Ford engine that powers the Elan.

A classic double overhead camshaft engine: the OSCA. One camshaft is under the coverplate with the OSCA name in the foreground, the other is on the far side of the working hands.

The whole process of loading the cylinders with fuel/air mixture is one of the most important single factors in engine performance. Valves must be as large as possible, to allow a big charge to pass through them. (Some large-bore engines use *two* intake valves per cylinder to accomplish this end.)

In addition to being as large as possible, intake valves in the high-speed engine must also be closed quickly and positively at the end of the intake cycle. The camshaft only opens the valves; closing is done by springs. If these springs are to close the valves before the fast-turning cam opens them again, they must be extremely powerful. The faster the engine is expected to turn, the more powerful the valve springs must be. The speed with which the valves can be closed by the springs is indeed a factor that limits the speed of most engines. When the valves can no longer be closed by their springs before they are opened again, a condition known as *valve float* arises. When the valves start to float, the engine has reached its absolute maximum speed (if

Multiple carburetion. Here: three dual-choke downdraft Weber carburetors atop a Ferrari engine.

other factors have not already halted its acceleration). If allowed to continue, valve float will damage or destroy the engine.

Mixing the fuel/air charge that will eventually reach the cylinders is the job of the carburetor. The carburetor uses air pressure to vaporize gasoline much as a spray gun uses air to vaporize insecticide. The vaporized gasoline and air are then carried via manifolds through intake ports and valves into the combustion chamber itself. The whole intake passage—manifold, ports, and area around the valves—must be as straight and smooth as possible. Roughness or bends in the passage can greatly reduce the amount of fuel/air mixture that can enter the combustion chamber. Moreover, the lengths of the passages must be as nearly equal as possible, to avoid "starving" the cylinders that are farthest from the carburetor.

The theoretically ideal way to keep the intake passages both straight and equal in length is to use as many carburetors as there are cylinders in the engine, each one connected directly to the intake port. But four or more carburetors are an awful handful to synchronize, as well as taking up a tremendous amount of space and eating up an awful lot of money. One way of solving this problem is to use half as many carburetors as there are cylinders and settle for intake passages that are only slightly longer than the one-carburetor-per-cylinder system requires. A second is by the use of the multithroat or multichoke carburetor. The multithroat carburetor (usually two or four throats) is actually a mating of either two or four carburetors so that they have some parts in common, but an individual throat for each of the cylinders fed. Most Alfa-Romeo and Ferrari engines employ multichoke carburetors—Italian Webers, the most widely used in racing.

In addition to all the refinements of valves, cams, intake passages, and carburetors, there is an additional method of cramming a maximum amount of fuel/air mixture into the combustion chamber: *supercharging*. In the unsupercharged engine the mixture is sucked or "pulled" into the combustion chamber by the action of the piston. The supercharger is simply a pump that compresses the mixture in the intake passage. When the valve opens to admit the charge into the combustion chamber, the mixture is pushed into the chamber by the pressure exerted by the supercharger, as well as being "sucked" in by the piston's action. More mixture is thus admitted to the chamber, with a proportional increase in power.

In practice the supercharger is little used in sports car racing. Most sets of racing regulations require that supercharged cars race in a displacement class larger than the actual displacement of the car. And the benefits gained by supercharging are rarely great enough to make such a handicap worth while. The supercharger adds weight and complexity to the sports car engine. Complexity invariably increases the chance of mechanical failures. And the very nature of supercharging—that of squeezing more out of an engine that it was originally designed to do—puts unplanned-for stresses on the engine, leading to equally unplanned breakdowns. So while the supercharger can be a useful and reliable adjunct to small, lightly stressed utility engines, it is not often used on the already-highly-stressed racing sports car engine.

A few modern engines do not use carburetors to mix the fuel/air charge, but instead rely on *fuel injection*. The purest form of fuel injection is found on the Mercedes-Benz 300SL. In this engine air alone is sucked into the engine by the action of the pistons, the fuel is injected (pumped) directly into the combustion chamber at the proper moment. The injection system used on the Corvette 327 engine is closer to conventional carburetion in that *both* fuel and air enter the engine through the intake valves. In the Corvette, however, the fuel is injected into the air in the intake passage just ahead of the valves, rather than mixed with it in a carburetor. Both methods of fuel injection are extremely successful but, because of the precise mechanisms required, are considerably more expensive than carburetion. It is likely that more and more engines will employ this system in the future.

Like all internal-combustion engines, sports car engines generate a great deal of heat and must be artificially cooled to prevent them from burning themselves out. The majority of sports car engines are water-cooled, with conventional radiator, coolant passages that run within the engines, and a fan to pull cooling air across the radiator at low speeds. Unfortunately, turning the fan uses up a considerable amount of horsepower, but because of the fans value at low speeds, this disadvantage is tolerated. The fan is often unnecessary at high speeds, when a great deal of air is being pushed through the radiator by the movement of the car itself. In some the fan has been dispensed with altogether. A long idle on the starting grid can be pretty tough on such an engine!

In addition to cooling the engine with water, many sports cars make provision for cooling the oil that circulates in the engine. An oversized, finned, light-metal sump is often employed, and in addition, the oil itself is often circulated through a small oil radiator in front of the water radiator.

A small minority of sports car engines uses air-cooling rather than water-cooling. Since among them is one of the most successful engines in all racing history (the Porsche), it is safe to assume that this method is as effective as water-cooling—at least on smaller (under 2000 cc.) engines. The air-cooled engine uses a large fan and a system of ducts to direct cooling air over the engine (primarily over the cylinder heads, where most engine heat is generated). Air-cooling has much to recommend it: simplicity, lightness, and reliability.

Ignition in sports car engines is of two types: coil and magneto. Most dual-purpose cars use coil ignition because it is (a) adequate and (b) less expensive than magneto ignition. At very high engine speeds, however, the coil begins to have trouble building up enough current for a good spark. It simply does not get the time it needs to do the job. Hence the magneto—a kind of high-voltage generator driven by the engine—is used on a number of high-speed, high-performance engines. Its output is proportional to engine speed. So the faster the engine turns, the more the magneto delivers—right when it is most needed. Since the magneto delivers sufficient voltage for a spark, no coil is necessary.

Two types of spark plugs are commonly used in racing. One is the "hot," or "soft," plug; the other the "cold," or "hard," plug. Confusingly enough, the hot plug is used for warming up a cold engine, the cold plug for hot, high-speed operation. One of the commonest sights in the paddock is that of a driver or mechanic switching from his warm-up plugs to the cold plugs he will use in the race itself.

The sports car clutch and gearbox must be rugged enough to stand up to the brutal treatment they receive in competition. For racing the clutch lining is generally of a material that engages less smoothly than that used for touring, but that will take considerably more hard wear. Gearboxes are of the four-speed (and very occasionally of the five-speed) type. Extra speeds are an advantage, since each one adds a road-speed range in which the engine can perform at its maximum output. Today's gearboxes are generally the synchromesh type, rather than the older "crash" type. The synchromesh gearbox permits down-shifting without double-clutching, where the "crash" box did not. In practice, however, a good deal of double-clutching is done even with the synchromesh box, to ease strains on the gears. In many gearboxes, first gear is not synchronized. It matters little, however, since low will be used only at the start. Gearshift levers are frequently fitted with a device that makes it impossible to shift into reverse by mistake during a race.

Brakes

Sports car brakes are fully as important as sports car engines. If this seems strange in a sport where speed is the objective, remember that on a winding sports car course, high over-all speeds can only be attained if brakes are adequate to slow the car for turns, slow it quickly, and slow it lap after lap after lap.

Consider this example: two cars of roughly equal speed and cornering ability, running neck-and-neck at 120 mph. on a long straight that ends in a sharp right-hand corner. Because of less effective brakes, or brakes that have been weakened through hard use, one car must start to brake 150 yards before the corner in order to get down to the speed at which the corner can be safely taken. The other car, with fundamentally superior braking, or with brakes that have stood up better to the strain of preceding laps, need start braking only 125 yards before the corner. That extra 25 yards of top speed obviously will make a winner out of car B every time.

Brakes stop a car by transforming its motion into heat. So brakes get HOT! This heat must be dissipated before it can work its unpleasant effects on the metals, fluids and other materials involved in the braking process.

The brakes used on modern sports cars are of two types: drum and disc. (Strictly speaking, what is commonly referred to as a disc brake is actually a "spot" or "caliper" brake—the true disc brake being a somewhat different animal. But the term "disc brake" is so widely used for the "spot" brake that its precise definition has become one used largely only by engineers.)

The drum brake is commonly used on all American passenger cars. It consists of a metal drum that revolves with the wheel, and a non-revolving set of brake shoes and linings that press against the inside of the drum during braking. Linings may be made of asbestos or other heat-resistant materials and blends of materials. The drum is frequently made of cast iron, a metal that provides excellent friction, but that conducts and dissipates heat poorly. A more advanced type of brake drum is constructed of aluminum, with an interior lining of cast iron bonded to it. Since aluminum has excellent properties of heat conductivity, it is ideal for carrying away heat. The exterior surface of the brake drum is flanged or finned to strengthen it and to give an even more heat-dissipating surface.

Because of its construction the drum brake is susceptible to a failing known as "brake fade"—a reduction or (in extreme cases) a complete

Drum brakes, outboard, on a Porsche. Note the fins which increase exterior surface area to promote cooling.

loss of stopping power. One cause of brake fade is expansion of the brake drum by heat. Such expansion may increase the distance between lining and drum to a point where the lining cannot press against the drum even when the brake pedal is fully depressed. However, good design, plenty of finning, and suitable air-ducting can do much to prevent fade. Nevertheless, in the modern sports car, drum brakes have been almost totally relegated to the rear wheels, where braking stresses are smallest.

Up front today, and often all around, are disc brakes. This fairly recent development is extraordinarily simple in principle. It consists of a metal disc that revolves with the wheel, and a pair of lined calipers that press against the two surfaces during braking. The process can be compared to squeezing the flat surfaces of a turning phonograph record with a pair of pliers. The disc brake is virtually fade-free, since no matter how much heat may expand the disc the disc can still be gripped by the calipers. It remains remarkably unaffected by mud or water, since gripping the disc cleans it on the first revolution. Of particular interest in long-distance racing is the fact that the pads (or lining) on the calipers can be quickly changed if worn.

Disc brakes proved their worth in racing as far back as 1953. In the historic Le Mans race that year, Jaguars ran away with the first three places, thanks largely to the efficiency of their then revolutionary disc brakes. The discs allowed the Jaguars to maintain speed far closer to each turn, and cut their lap time accordingly. Since that year, disc brakes have become almost totally accepted among sports car manufacturers. Four-wheel disc brakes are used on all of today's Ferraris, Porsches, Cobras, and Corvettes. Front disc brakes are used today even on most low-priced sports cars, and rear discs are optional on several cars with front discs (Healey 3000 and Volvo.)

Whether disc or drum, brakes may be located either at the wheels of the car (outboard) or at the center of the car (inboard). The most common location is at the wheels, where they are closer to the cooling air. However, inboard rear brakes are quite common and completely practical. One real advantage of inboard brakes is a reduction in unsprung weight (see Suspension, below). Difficulties in cooling inboard brakes can be largely overcome by proper air-ducting, and of course the newer disc brake is less affected by heat than is the drum. Inboard rear brakes may often be found in such sports-racing designs as the Lotus, Elva, Lola, and rear-engined Ferraris.

Suspension

The sports car's suspension is another of the important factors that affect a car's performance. Raw power and potent braking are important but useless unless they are tamed. As the enthusiast says, a car must "handle" well. Good handling depends on proper weight distribution, responsive steering, and a number of other factors. But unquestionably the most important factor is the car's suspension.

A car touches the road at just four points—four small areas of tire of its wheels. Everything else in the car is suspended from those wheels. Hence the word "suspension." In other language, a car's suspension consists of the way the rest of the car is connected with the wheels. Thus suspension concerns springing, axle design, shock absorbers, and the like.

All modern sports cars have *independent* front-wheel suspension. Many have independent rear-wheel suspension, too. When wheels are independently suspended, neither interacts with the other. When a right-hand wheel goes over a bump, the left-hand wheel isn't affected at all. Because of this tendency for one wheel to stay on the ground even when its opposite number is up in the air, independent suspension is generally conceded to be the ultimate type of suspension. Some fine performers get along without independent rear suspension (Alfa Romeo), but some otherwise-fine cars have suffered from the lack of it (D-Jaguar).

Up front, independent suspension is easy to attain. In all but a few designs, front wheels do no driving, so there is no need for them to be interconnected with the differential and power train. Each wheel can be easily sprung—by coil spring or torsion bars in most modern sports cars. Shock absorbers (usually tubular and often enclosed by coil springs) are of course used. For racing shock absorbers are usually considerably "stiffer" than for normal driving, to prevent the wheel from needless bouncing around under competitive stresses.

A primary object of both front- and rear-suspension design is to keep as much of the weight of the car as possible suspended on the springs, rather than having it tied rigidly to the wheels. When a great deal of weight is rigidly connected to the wheels, they are certain to bound and rebound more violently on bumps and rough spots, causing temporary losses of adhesion. Since loss of adhesion (the failure of tires to stick to the road) is obviously to be avoided like the plague, modern designers make the reduction of unsprung weight a primary objective.

In an extreme attempt to cut unsprung weight, a few ounces have been shaved by drilling metal from this knock-off hub cap.

While the reduction of unsprung weight in the front is largely a matter of paring the weight of wheels, brakes, and suspension arms to a minimum, it is more complicated in the rear. For the rear wheels must, in addition to turning and stopping, receive power from the engine . . . via gearbox, drive shaft, differential, and axles.

The commonest way of transmitting this power to the wheels is via a "live" rear axle. This method of non-independent rear suspension consists of a rigid, hollow axle housing that extends from one wheel to the other and contains an inner axle shaft on each side of a centrally located differential. These shafts transmit power from the differential to the wheels. The two major disadvantages of the live rear axle are (1) a great deal of unsprung weight and (2) the rigid interconnection of the two rear wheels so that all rising or falling action of one rear wheel gives rise to complementary action in the other wheel.

Despite these undesirable features a number of fine, expensive sports cars, as well as most low- and medium-priced dual-purpose cars, manage to get along with the "live" rear axle. Properly designed, it can be remarkably successful—as proved by its use on the 250 GT Ferraris and many Alfa Romeos.

The next step toward fully independent rear suspension is the De Dion rear suspension. In the De Dion rear end the differential is rigidly attached to the frame of the car, for a great reduction in unsprung weight. The two rear wheels are rigidly connected, one to the other, by a hollow tube, called the De Dion tube. Power gets from differential to wheels via universally jointed unenclosed axles. Brakes may be located either at the wheel or, for a further reduction in unsprung weight, inboard near the differential. The De Dion rear suspension is not often used in modern sports cars, but at one time was most successful in Maseratis, Lister-Jaguars, and Ferraris.

Fully independent rear suspension is attained when the two rear wheels have no rigid connection with one another—neither the axle casing of the "live" rear end nor the De Dion tube. Thus the bound and rebound of one rear wheel can have no effect on the other. With fully independent rear suspension, as with the De Dion design, the differential (and transmission too, if it is located in the rear) is rigidly attached to the frame of the car. The wheels are driven from the differential by means of axle shafts. The wheels are located with regard to the chassis by pivoted arms, leaf springs, wishbones or other devices. Because of the motion of the wheels relative to the differential, the shafts must include universal joints—either one or two per shaft, depending on design. The variations of independent rear suspension

Fully independent rear suspension
Cooper Formula III style, with wishbone
below axles, leaf springs above
Chain drive is typical of Formula III car
but is found nowhere else among
racing automobiles today

De Dion rear suspension on a Lister-Bristol. Thick curved tube is De Dion tube connecting the two rear wheels. Note how differential is rigidly attached to tubular frame members. Inboard disc brakes can be seen at either side of differential.

are too numerous to describe here. But one or another is used in practically all modern sports-racing cars: Cobra, Porsche, Ferrari, Ford GT. Independent rear suspension has also found its way into a number of mass-produced sports cars: Triumph Spitfires and Jaguar XK-E's. Production Porsches have had it since Day One. And in 1963, Corvette went fully independent, as did the Triumph TR4A in 1965.

Body and Frame

Most sports cars employ separate body and frame. (Production Porsches are one outstanding exception.) In the less expensive dual-purpose cars the frame consists of several relatively heavy steel girders, atop which sits the body. While this method of frame construction is simple and cheap, it is not the best in terms of either lightness or rigidity.

The tubular frame, made up of a number of steel tubes ranging from ½″ to 2″ or more in diameter, is both lighter and more rigid (particularly with regard to twisting forces) than the girder frame. The tubes are welded together, and often extend up into the body of the car. When the upper tubes play an important role in the over-all rigidity of the frame (rather than just serving as members from which to hang the body), and all tubes are stressed, the frame is known as a "space frame." A number of racing sports cars employ the tubular frame . . . among them the Alfa GTZ and the McLaren-Elva.

Current design trends seem to be running away from the separate body and frame. The Porsche, of course, has had a unitized body and frame for years, and the current 911 and 912 continue this construction method. There are no independent frame members in these Porsches. Everything is of sheet metal, and is welded to the body in such a way that the entire structure—not just the frame—supports both mechanical components and passengers. Such construction has one disadvantage: it is rather difficult to repair when badly damaged. A collision that would probably require only expensive sheet-metal repair on a conventional car may make a total loss of a Porsche. But unitized construction continues to make inroads. Even a relatively conventional Detroit product like the Mustang now boasts it.

The body of the sports car may be of steel, light metal (magnesium or aluminum), or fiberglass. Steel is strong and cheap, but heavy. Most dual-purpose cars use it. Aluminum or magnesium cut many pounds from body weight, and are used in many racing sports cars. Light metals are easily damaged and often difficult to repair, but are worth their disadvantages because of the weight they save. Fiberglass is also much lighter than steel, and in a production car can be most success-ful: witness the Corvette. A good fiberglass body requires costly molds to shape it, hence is seldom feasible for the one-of-a-kind sports car "special" unless purchased ready-made from a fiberglass body manu-facturer. Unlike metal, fiberglass has a tendency to crack and break rather than bend. Minor repairs are easy with fiberglass, major ones pretty rugged.

Fully as important as the *lightness* of the sports car body is its *stream-lining*. For just as excess weight eats up horsepower that could be push-ing the car faster, so does a lack of streamlining. A small frontal area is particularly important in keeping air resistance low (a great deal of the success of the Lola, Lotus, and Elva can be traced to their tiny frontal area and generally excellent aerodynamic design). Streamlining the underside of the car is just as important as the streamlining that meets the eye. A smooth underbelly can add a number of miles per hour to a car's top speed. Since air resistance increases at a rate that is more than proportional to speed, functional streamlining becomes increas-ingly important as the speed of the car goes up.

The cockpit of the sports car should of course be comfortable, so that the driver can devote all of his energy to driving. Particularly in a long race, fatigue can sap a driver's strength and skill in a disastrous way. The bucket seat contributes much to his comfort, by holding him firmly in position during severe cornering. The safety belt, in addition to the crash protection it provides, also helps the driver stay in a comfortable driving position.

The indispensable instrument in the sports car cockpit is the *tachome-ter*. It shows the speed at which the *engine* is turning, and is a "must" for competition driving, where the engine must do its utmost in every gear. The tachometer must be large and legible so that it can be read at a glance. For racing purposes the speedometer is rarely used. A racing driver is interested, not in his speed, but rather in the efficiency with which his engine is performing. The tachometer tells him that.

The racing cockpit, stark and functional. Large, indispensable tachometer enjoys place of honor directly in front of driver.

The second most important instrument in the car is its oil-pressure gauge, which tells the driver whether oil is being pushed around to various points in the engine at the proper pressure. A drop in oil pressure is the surest sign that an engine is about to do itself harm. The oil-pressure gauge should be a real, honest-to-goodness *gauge*—one that shows up trouble when it starts, not after it's happened. A warning light is no substitute for a gauge.

Water- and oil-temperature gauges come next in importance. Better to detect engine overheating by glancing at a gauge than by screeching to a halt with a seized-up engine. A charge indicator should also be in the cockpit to tell the driver whether his generator is doing its job.

Dual-Purpose and Racing Sports Cars

Regardless of individual design features, virtually all sports cars can be placed into one of two major categories. These are (1) the "dual-purpose" sports cars and (2) the racing sports cars. Knowing the difference between the two types makes it easy to understand why an 1100 cc. Lotus can trim an Austin-Healey 3000 whose engine is almost three times its size.

The dual-purpose sports car has (surprise) *two* purposes. One is *sport* —racing, rallying, hill-climbing. The other is *utility*. Comfortable high-speed touring. Shopping. Driving in traffic. Commuting. And even carrying some luggage once in a while . . . not much, but some.

The racing sports car is a different breed of cat. It is a mono-purpose car: for racing only. You would hardly be comfortable touring in a Lola. Or driving to the station in a Ferrari 330P. Or inching through traffic in your Chaparral. All that keeps these cars from being all-out racing types like Grand Prix or Indianapolis cars is features that have been added mostly to qualify them as sports cars: lights, batteries, tops that can conceivably keep out rain, self-starters, spare tires, and a passenger seat that frequently meets only legal, not human requirements.

For practical purposes you can pretty much distinguish the two types by their classification as "production" or "modified." Cars that race in the production category are almost always dual-purpose sports cars; cars that race "modified" are almost always racing sports cars. While it is true that many production cars arrive at the course on trailers, and could hardly run to the station in their sharp state of racing tune, these cars do qualify as dual-purpose cars simply because the intent of their builders was to make them such. Detuned, they could again be everyday, go-to-market, dual-purpose sports cars.

But no matter how "dual" the purposes for which a production car is designed, it must be considerably modified if it is to be a winner on the race course. The man who enters his newly purchased, unmodified MG in a race will soon discover (long before the first lap is over) that some MG's are more "production" than others! But what is the difference? Isn't his MG a production MG? Aren't the others listed as production MG's too? Then how come they're so much faster?

The answer lies in the fact that "production," in racing, does not really *mean* production. It does mean that a certain number of a particular car have been produced. And it does mean that the modifications that can be performed on the car are strictly limited: in nature, in degree. Some modifications to production cars require new parts (gears, for example). Most of these must be catalogued by the manufacturer of the car as regular production options. Most cannot be "hop-up" items produced by other manufacturers, or by a local machine shop. To this extent, therefore, "production" cars *are* truly production. But the permissible modifications are great enough to make a remarkable difference in the car's performance. "Prodified" is the expression for a production car that has been modified to just this side of illegality.

What modifications are permissible? The SCCA rules that the following alterations (and some others) can be made on a production car without disqualifying it from the production category.

1. New brake lining may be installed . . . tougher, harder linings that make prolonged, severe braking possible.
2. New clutch linings and springs may be installed . . . components which will better withstand the shock of racing gear-changes.
3. Racing tires may (and in the case of high-speed cars *must*) be installed. Lives depend on them.
4. "Stiffer" shock absorbers may be installed, to improve handling.
5. Various types of spark plugs may be used—high-speed competition and around-town touring make entirely different demands on plugs. Make and type of ignition coil may be changed, too.
6. Carburetors or fuel-injection mechanism may be altered, but not replaced. Number, model, type, or size of unit must remain unchanged. But this modification can amount to an almost complete rebuild.
7. Engine components may be lightened or modified. Such components include valves, head, camshaft, and rods. Compression ratio may be raised. Intake and exhaust ports may be matched and polished. Stronger valve springs may be installed. But no metal may be added to original components. Any make or type of piston may be installed.
8. Gearbox ratios may be altered. Another very vital modification. Low gear on many cars, for example, is designed to move the car up

the steepest hills, starting from a standstill. Obviously this is a condition that is never encountered in racing.

9. Rear-axle gear ratios may be altered. Generally speaking, the gear is altered in such a way that the car's top speed on a given course is matched to maximum engine rpm. Remember: acceleration and top speed are mutual enemies as far as gearing is concerned. It's no good having an axle ratio that allows 125 mph. if you're driving on a short, twisty course that never lets you exceed 90 mph. Better to sacrifice useless top speed and switch to an axle ratio that gives better acceleration coming out of the corners.

10. Balancing is permitted. Each of the engine's pistons and connecting rods may be lightened or weighted until all weigh exactly the same. Crankshafts and other rotary parts may be adjusted until their balance around their axes is perfect. Manufacturers' tolerances in these areas can almost always be improved on. So doing can pay big dividends in engine life under the stress of racing.

11. Windshields may be removed and replaced with a small air screen. This makes little difference at low speed, but at high speed the reduction in air resistance makes a great deal.

12. Straight exhaust pipes (with no muffler) may be used.

13. Weight of the entire car may be reduced 5 per cent from stock. In a Corvette, for example, this will take off some 150 pounds.

14. Strengthening of wheels is both permitted and encouraged.

With racing sports or modified cars the question of "permissible modifications" does not arise. These cars need only meet the sanctioning organization's definition of a "sports car." This definition may consist of a seating requirement (two, side by side of such-and-such a size), a real door of specified size, windscreen, complete electrical system (starter, lights, etc.), minimum ground clearance, maximum turning circle, requirements of a spare tire, a "pump" fuel requirement, and so on. Outside of this, anything—or almost anything—goes. Only one modification is penalized: the supercharger.

Thousands of sports cars—production and modified—are raced every year in the U.S. The following pages are designed to introduce most of the important cars—important either in number or in performance or both. It is unfortunate that there is no room in a book of this kind for the many one-of-a-kind "specials" so devotedly built and raced. But there is not. In addition to the general information about the cars that *are* covered there is a brief list of specifications. Included among these are:

Engine. Number of cylinders and how arranged, if other than in-line. Method by which valves are operated: push-rod overhead valves (OHV), single overhead camshaft (SOHC), or double overhead camshaft (DOHC). Brake horsepower (bhp.): in the case of production cars, the stock manufacturer's figure is given. This figure is considerably smaller than that which a well-tuned and suitably "prodified" engine will deliver . . . perhaps as little as 75 per cent of it. In the case of modified cars, too, owner modifications and tuning may increase the horsepower originally built into the engine by the manufacturer. Displacement in cubic centimeters (cc.)

Weight. An important figure, since a car's weight-to-horsepower ratio is a primary measure of its potential. Approximate curb weights (full load of gas, oil, and water) are given for production cars, approximate dry weights for modified cars.

Acceleration. A rough estimate of the number of seconds it takes a car to reach 60 mph. from a standing start, based on published figures in American and European motoring publications. Remember that gearing can significantly alter these figures. While 0–60 is the most common acceleration yardstick, other figures (80–100) may also be significant. Generally speaking, however, a car that's fast from 0 to 60 will do well at in the higher ranges, too.

Top speed. In the case of production cars, this figure is approximately the correct one with the stock engine and standard rear axle. "Prodified" cars will of course do considerably over this "maximum."

But enough explanations. Here are the cars!

ALFA ROMEO (Italian)

ALFA ROMEO GIULA VELOCE SPIDER

Engine: 4 cyl. DOHC   1570 cc.   129 bhp.

2140 pounds   0–60: 10 secs.   Max. speed: 110 mph.

For over a decade, the design of Alfa small-bore sports cars has remained remarkably consistent. 4-cylinder double overhead cam engine mounted up front and a "live" rear axle may not be the most modern

Leaning, but hanging on, an Alfa Spider corners. This 1300 cc. model is almost indistinguishable from the newer 1600 cc. models.

way of building a sports car, but in the Alfa, it's certainly proved to be one of the most effective.

Starting in 1956, the small Alfa production engine was set at 1300 cc. But in 1963, the engine was slightly bored and stroked to increase the displacement to 1570 cc. The most powerful production version of the engine delivers 129 bhp. This engine lies under the hood of both the Giula Veloce Spider (the roadster) and the Giula Sprint GT (coupe). Both cars are potent performers, although the convertible is the most popular choice for serious racing. Not surprisingly, the roadster has slightly better acceleration than the coupe (because it is a bit lighter). But in turn, the coupe's top speed betters that of the roadster (because its smooth top offers less wind resistance at high speeds).

The Giula's DOHC engine is a study in classic high-performance small engines. Five main bearings allow plenty of crankshaft revs without breaking anything. The cylinders are fed by two sidedraft twin-choke Weber carburetors. While the engine's output is not astounding for its size (a bit over 80 bhp. per liter), it can be tuned to deliver well over 100 bhp. per liter.

The 1600 cc. Alfa differs from its 1300 cc. predecessors in two other important respects. A 5-speed transmission (quite a novelty in a production sports car) replaces the older 4-speed. And Alfa has finally gotten the disc brake idea. Long a holdout for drums (albeit good ones), Alfa now fits front discs to the Giula Veloce. (Discs all around mark the Giula Sprint GT).

Coil springs are used at all four wheels on the Giula. The live rear axle may seem out of place in an automotive world which is moving more and more toward independent rear suspensions—but criticisms of the Alfa's road-holding are few and far between. Bodies of both coupe and convertible are beautifully finished steel.

Both coupe and convertible are available with less powerful engines (104 bhp.) that have but a single Solex twin-choke carburetor. These compete in a lower class than the 129 bhp. versions.

It's difficult to distinguish the older 1300 cc. Spider from the newer 1600 model by looks alone. But the presence of small but distinct air scoop on the hood of a Spider definitely marks it as a 1600.

Alfa's exciting contribution to Gran Turismo racing: the GTZ.

ALFA ROMEO GTZ

Engine: 4 cyl. DOHC	1570 cc.	150 bhp.
Approx. 1500 pounds	0–60: 7.5 secs.	Max. speed: 140 mph.

This is what happens when Alfa really sets out to go racing. Based on the Spider Veloce, and classified by the SCCA as a production car, the GTZ has little to do with either.

Start with the frame—a complex, multi-tube space frame which earned the car its Italian nickname of "Tubolare." Up front is the familiar 1570 cc. engine, tuned by the factory to put out 150 bhp.; by independent Italian modifiers to as much as 175 bhp. And in the rear, no live axle to hop and skip. Instead, there's fully independent rear suspension—quite a departure in an Alfa sports car. A light alloy body and four-wheel disc brakes complete this effective sports racer.

The "GT" stands for Grand Touring—but it's a touring car only in a racing sense. The "Z" is Zagato, an Italian body-builder who wrapped up this pretty package. You can put one in your garage for about $9000. On weekends, you can drive it to spots like Sebring. If you'd been there in 1964 or 1965, for example, you'd have seen your GTZ's twins mop up absolutely everything in their class.

A popular Vee—the Autodynamics.

AUTODYNAMICS (American)

AUTODYNAMICS FORMULA VEE

Engine: 4 cyl. OHV (Volkswagen)   1192 cc.   45 bhp. (app.)

825 pounds   0–60: 14 secs. (app.)   Max. speed: 110 mph.

One of the most popular Vees, the Autodynamics car wrapped up the 1964 championship in the hands of designer Ray Caldwell; racked up more points than any other Vee in the 1965 season.

Since Vee regulations are very stringent, all Vees sound pretty much alike when described. The Autodynamics is typical. The frame is tubular steel, covered by a three-piece Fiberglas body. Front suspension is fairly stock VW, except for the replacement of the lower torsion bar with a roll bar. At the rear, the VW torsion bars have been discarded in favor of coil springs.

Light weight (minimum weight limit for Vees is 900 pounds lower than the weight of a stock VW sedan) and good aerodynamics make the car capable of lap times approaching those of C production cars.

The big appeal of Vees is the opportunity they afford to own and drive an open-wheeled racing car for very little money. An Autodynamics kit costs $995. All you need in addition is enough wrecked VW to supply engine, suspension, steering and transaxle. These, plus racing tires and a lot of loving assembly and tuning, are all you need to go racing in one of the most closely contested classes in America.

AUSTIN-HEALEY (British)

AUSTIN-HEALEY SPRITE

Engine: 4 cyl. OHV	1098 cc.	55 bhp.
1550 pounds	0–60: 18 secs.	Max. speed: 90 mph.

This baby sister of the big Austin-Healeys is one of the most-raced cars on American courses. One very good reason for the Sprite's popularity is her low price—about $1900. Helping hold down that price is the fact that many of her components are those used in several small English family cars. Her engine is basically that of the Morris 1100 and MG 1100 Sports Sedan. Her rear axle and coil springs were originally Austin, her steering originally Morris Minor.

Straightforward is the word for the Sprite's design. It's rugged and well-proved. The steel body will withstand plenty of punishment; the front disc brakes, plenty of hard stopping. Her price and reliability have made her just about the standard beginner's car for racing.

Don't be surprised if you see Sprites competing in more than one class. The earliest Sprites had 948 cc. engines, and unless equipped with many options, can't match the 1100's.

AUSTIN-HEALEY 100-6

Engine: 6 cyl. OHV	2639 cc.	117 bhp.
2600 pounds	0–60: 10½ secs.	Max. speed: 110 mph.

The performance of this Austin-Healey is just about on a par with that of the earlier four-cylinder Austin-Healey 100, but below that of the limited production, aluminum-bodied four-cylinder 100S, in which 132 horses pushed a car weighing about 2100 pounds. Like all the Healeys, the 100-6 is a fast, dependable, good-looking machine much seen on American courses. Its relatively low price has contributed greatly to its popularity. While the car has no particularly outstanding mechanical features, it combines much that is tried, reliable, and successful in modern sports car design. Healey competition is hot and

Bug-eyed look marked this early Sprite. Newer models are far sleeker.

AUSTIN-HEALEY 3000 (Mark III)

Engine: 6 cyl. OHV   2912 cc.   148 bhp.
2600 pounds   0–60: 9.5 secs.   Max. speed: 115 mph.

Last of a line that started in the early Fifties, the 3000 boasts 25% more power than the 100-6. Disc brakes are standard equipment on front wheels, optional on rear wheels. As in most of its stablemates from British Motors (Sprites, MGB's, MG 1100's), the engine is front-mounted, the rear suspension is "live."

Most of the competition in the Healey's class is pretty tough for this car to handle. But a well-prepared, well-driven one can usually put up a good fight. And since, like the 100-6, it's a popular car, there's almost always a good battle among the 3000's.

Two 100-6's find the same line through a corner.

Lively, yes; lovely, no. "Wings" at lower edge of Chaparral's front fenders help prevent front end lift at high speeds.

CHAPARRAL (American)

CHAPARRAL II

Engine: V-8 OHV	5400 cc.	Approx. 425 bhp.
1600 pounds	0–60: 5 secs. (est.)	Max. speed: 180 mph.

Every year, dozens of one-of-a-kind "specials"—cars turned out not by a factory but built by a few loving hands—make their debuts on American courses. Most disappear as abruptly as they appear, simply because they are ill-built or ill-conceived. The brains, wallet, and work-shop of the average "special" builder are simply no match for those of Porsche, Ferrari, Lotus, and other manufacturers.

But occasionally a "special" appears that's a real giant killer. Usually, it's a product of more money and skill than the average backyard builder can muster. A product like the three Scarabs built by Reventlow Auto-mobiles in the late fifties.

Or, to bring matters more up to date, a car like the fantastic Chaparral II, built near Midland, Texas, in a small factory that just happens to have a two-mile racing test track in its backyard.

The Chaparral's list of racing triumphs is lengthy . . . highlighted by winning the USRRC championship in 1964, and coming within an ace of doing so again in 1965. But it is crowned by an over-all victory at Sebring in 1965—clipping 9 seconds off the lap record in practice; finishing twenty miles ahead of the second-place winner. At Sebring, it ran against the very best the world has to offer.

Two highly unusual features mark the Chaparral II—a Fiberglas frame and an automatic transmission. The frame consists of almost a dozen Fiberglas-reinforced plastic units, bonded together to form an extremely light and rigid unit. In a way, the whole car's just a big plastic box.

The automatic transmission is based on a GM unit, and has proved tremendously effective. It's easy on the engine, because it totally prevents missed shifts and murderous over-revving. And it's even easier on the driver—because it eliminates a lot of work. No clutching, no shifting— just steer (with *both* hands), brake, and accelerate.

The Chaparral II is powered by a rear-mounted, much-modified Chevrolet 327 cu. inch engine. Four twin-choke Weber carburetors supply the fuel/air mixture. Brakes are outboard discs at all four wheels. Suspension is fully independent all around, and owes much to Lotus practice. Great big 15″ tires put the power on the pavement. All in all, enough car to make even Enzo Ferrari sit up and take notice.

CHEVROLET (American)

CORVETTE STING RAY 396

Engine: V-8 OHV	6488 cc.	425 bhp.
3200 pounds	0–60: 6 secs.	Max. speed: 135 mph.

Dragsters . . . hot-rods . . . jalopies . . . midgets . . . Indianapolis cars . . . stock cars . . . the United States has 'em all in abundance. But sports cars? *Just one:* the Chevrolet Corvette.

Sad that in this country—the world's most "automobilized"—this is so. But where distances are so great, and highways so wide and straight, manufacturers have naturally emphasized the big, comfortable touring car. That such cars tend to have poorer handling characteristics than the smaller, more agile sports car is an established fact. But Americans, accustomed to regarding the automobile as a necessary work horse, have, until recently, simply never demanded a car that would behave as a sporting implement.

But we *do* have the Corvette. In one way, at least, it's typically American. It's BIG . . . in length and weight and width and engine size.

The Corvette's performance is big, too. With an engine of over 6 liters, it ought to be. A big 4-barrel carburetor feeds this engine, and a four-speed transmission backs it up. Suspension is fully independent, with coil springs at the front, leaf springs at the back. And she's the first American car with disc brakes at all four wheels. All Sting Rays carry Fiberglas bodies—the only American production car to do so. Beneath the body is a steel ladder-type frame.

A considerable variety of Corvettes are raced. One with a 427 cu. inch (7000 cc.) engine. Or a 327 cu. inch (5360 cc.) fuel-injected engine may lurk beneath that Fiberglas hood. In the case of the pre-Sting Ray (1963) models, a 283 cu. inch (4637 cc.) fuel-injected engine may be developing the power (approx. 315 bhp.). Prior to the 1963 models, Corvettes had neither disc brakes nor independent rear suspension.

Non-stock scoop on this Sting Ray's hood covers carburetor air intakes.

Lines of the Daimler are choppy, but her V-8's performance is smooth.

DAIMLER (British)

DAIMLER SP 250

Engine: V-8 OHV	2548 cc.	140 bhp.
2250 pounds	0–60: 9 secs.	Max. speed: 125 mph.

Try this on any enthusiast: ask him to name *two* production sports cars with V-8 engines, fiberglass bodies, and live rear axles. Chances are there'll be a long pause after he's said "Corvette." If he comes up with the Daimler SP 250 as number two, give him high marks. For this British car is relatively unfamiliar here.

Though its looks are rather unpleasing to many eyes, the Daimler's performance is anything but. The big (for an English sports car) V-8 is smooth, durable, and powerful. Disc brakes on all four wheels give the car stopping power to match its performance.

In its debut year in America (1960), the Daimler was rather pessimistically placed in Class E. One particularly well-prepared SP 250 promptly proceeded to mop up all surrounding Alfas, Porsches, and Healeys—finishing first in class for the year with more than twice the points of the second-place car. To correct such an obvious misclassification, the SCCA moved the Daimler into more competitive classes in following seasons. Today, relatively few Daimlers are seen on American courses.

Following modern trend, Elva VI is rear-engined.

ELVA (British)

ELVA MARK VI		CLASS G MODIFIED
Engine: 4 cyl. SOHC	1150 cc.	105 bhp.
870 pounds	0–60: 8 secs. (est.)	Max. speed: 140 mph.

The Elva is one third of the all-British triumvirate that makes G Modified the exciting class it is. Lotus and Lola are the other two thirds. As in the Lotus and Lola, the Elva's power plant is the four-may be either a 4-cyl. SOHC Coventry-Climax (as in the specifications above) or one of several Cosworth-modified Fords. Suspension is independent, with coil springs and lower wishbones at the rear, the axle shafts acting as the upper wishbones. Brakes are drum, mounted inboard at the rear. A tubular frame supports an aluminum or aluminum and fiberglass body. All in all, a light little, fast little British racing sports car. Her name, aptly derived from the French *"elle va,"* sums her up. *She goes!*

ELVA COURIER		
Engine: 4-cyl. OHV	1622 cc.	90 bhp.
1500 pounds (dry)	0–60: 10½ secs.	Max. speed: 108 mph.

If Elva has a "production" model, it is the Fiberglas-bodied Courier. The Courier was originally powered by the BMC 1500 cc. engine of the first MGA's, but later got a boost from the MGA 1600 Mark II 1622 cc. engine. Gearbox in this Courier is also MGA. The frame is of simple, large-diameter tube construction. A live rear axle is used. Rear brakes

Elva Courier's Fiberglas body may cover either MG or British Ford engine, plus a number of other production car components.

are drum, front are discs. More recent Couriers may boast the 1800 cc. engine of the MGB, or a much-modified British Ford engine of 1500 cc. And the latest cars have independent suspension front and rear. With such a variety of engines and components lurking under the Fiberglas, it's no surprise that Couriers race in more than one class.

MCLAREN ELVA

Engine: V-8 OHV (Olds)	4500 cc.	350 bhp.
1300 pounds	0–60: 5 secs. (est.)	Max. speed: 175 mph. (est.)

Bruce McLaren, the young Grand Prix driver from New Zealand, designed it, Elva builds it in England. The car is an excellent example of current big-modified sports racers, and can be fitted with any one of several rumbling American V-8's: the Ford 289, the Chevy 327, or the bored-and-stroked Olds F-85 engine listed in the specifications above.

The McLaren-Elva's frame is tubular steel, with magnesium bulkheads for additional stiffening. Engine is rear-mounted, of course, with radiator mounted low up front to give a small frontal area. Suspension is fully independent, and there are Girling disc brakes at all four wheels. About $11,000 will buy you one of these cars—*without* engine. Put 350 or 400 horsepower into it, and you'll be able to go Chaparral hunting with more than a little chance of success.

A Chevy V-8 in wolf's clothing: the very competitive McLaren-Elva.

FERRARI (Italian)

Probably no manufacturer's name—or product—is more famous in the postwar automobile racing world than that of Enzo Ferrari. In recent years more of the world's winning racing and sports cars have come from his relatively small factory (near Bologna in northern Italy) than from any other.

Most racing Ferraris are hand-built, a few at a time, to suit the needs and designs of the moment. Even the touring cars he builds in somewhat larger numbers are far from being mass-produced in the Detroit sense of the word. Most Ferraris race in the modified classes—simply because there are seldom enough of any one model built to meet production-class requirements. Notable exceptions are the 250 GT Berlinetta, Coupe and California Convertible, the 250 GTO and the 275 GTB.

Son of GTO: the lean and handsome front-engined Ferrari GTB.

FERRARI 275 GTB

Engine: V-12 SOHC (2)	3286 cc.	300 bhp.
2420 pounds	0–60: 6 secs. (est.)	Max. speed: 170 mph.

Classified as a production car by the SCCA in 1966, the GTB may well be the last of the front-engined Ferrari GT racing cars. The 3.3 liter engine is a slightly bored-out version of the 3 liter V-12 which served Ferrari so well in the earlier 250 GTO. The engine is fed by six double-throat Weber downdraft carburetors. While the engine output is not astounding by today's standards, 1.5 horsepower per cubic inch of engine displacement is the sign of a *very* efficient engine.

The 5-speed transmission of the GTB is at the rear of the car, in a single unit with the differential. There are disc brakes at all four wheels. Suspension is fully independent with coil springs. The frame of the car is of tubular steel, with a steel body. This is strictly a two-seater in the old GT tradition . . . spare wheel and gas tanks (oversized for long-distance races) taking up all but minimal luggage space behind the two seats.

The GTB is an extremely impressive performer. If it is not often seen on American courses, it is because the car is built in limited quantities. And because, good as it is, the rear-engined Ferrari GT's are even better.

Ferrari 250 LM (Le Mans.) Grand touring, strictly race-bred.

FERRARI 250 LM

Engine: V-12 SOHC (2)	3286 cc.	320 bhp.
1870 pounds	0–60: 5½ secs. (est.)	Max. speed: 187 mph.

This car is the shape of the future (the late Sixties, anyhow) at Ferrari. While front-engine touring Ferraris will no doubt continue to be built, the rear-engined coupe and roadster are now the leaders of the Ferrari racing pack.

If it took Ferrari a long time to learn the rear-engined lesson, it was simply because his front-engined designs were so incredibly successful. But the new rear-engined Ferraris are proving themselves still more successful—even against ever-stiffening opposition.

The familiar 3.3 liter V-12 powers the 250 LM, sitting directly behind the driver's seat, ahead of the transmission and rear axle. As in the GTB, carburetion is by six double Webers. A higher compression ratio and various detail modifications account for the 250 LM's slightly greater power. As in the GTB, the power is handled by a 5-speed gearbox. But the 250 LM's box is unsynchronized, while the GTB's is fully synchronized.

A tubular steel frame and an aluminum body built by Scagliatti account for the 250 LM's light weight. All brakes are disc, and four-wheel independent suspension is used. A 35-gallon gas tank testifies that this car is all business: the long-distance racing business.

330P is typical Ferrari rear-engined roadster design.

FERRARI 330P

Engine: V-12 SOHC (2)　　　3967 cc.　　　370 bhp.

1730 pounds　　　0–60: 5 secs. (est.)　　　Max. speed: 190 mph.

Take the roof off a 250 LM, put a bigger engine in it, and you've got a 330P, more or less. The "P" stands for "Prototype"—which means that not enough of these cars were built to qualify for one of the more restricted classifications under FIA rules.

Once again, the engine is the old-faithful V-12, stretched out now to 4 liters. Perhaps the additional stretching wore the engine's reliability a little thin. Ferrari prototypes powered by the 3.3 liter V-12 generally outran or outlasted the 330P's in 1964, a year when both were running side by side.

In all respects except minor ones, the design features of the 330P are like those of the 250 LM. More power and less weight are the secrets of its increased performance. The 190 mph. top speed is *not* an example of Italian wishful thinking. A 330P was actually timed at that speed at Le Mans in 1964.

Pushing beyond the 330P, Ferrari has designed an entirely new car, designated the 330P2. The 330P2 is powered by a 4-liter engine of quite different design from the 330P. This engine has double overhead cam-shafts—for a total of four. A fine example of the 330P2's prowess was given at the Nuerburgring in 1965—where it ran roughshod over all competition—including four Ford GT4O's.

This is a Fiat? Scoop on rear deck catches cool air, directs it to rear-mounted Fiat-Abarth engine.

FIAT-ABARTH (Italian)

FIAT-ABARTH-ZAGATO		CLASS G PRODUCTION
Engine: 4 cyl. OHV	747 cc.	50 bhp.
1200 pounds	0–60: 15 secs.	Max. speed: 90 mph.

Back to front the name breaks down like this: body by Zagato, engine modifications by Abarth, basic engine by Fiat.

The "engine modifications" amount to an almost complete rebuild of the 600 cc. engine that powers Fiat's stubby little sedan. Look what's been done to it: Displacement increased 25 per cent—from 600 to 750 cc. Compression increased from 7:1 to almost 10:1. Radical changes made in carburetion, camshaft, flywheel, cooling and exhaust systems. The result: horsepower more than doubled!

As if this weren't enough, this modified engine runs a car that's about a hundred pounds lighter than the Fiat 600, and carries a beautifully streamlined coupe body. (Like many Fiat-Abarth engines, this one is also available in a roadster designed by Allemano.) All this is the brain child of designer Carlo Abarth, one of the true automotive geniuses of modern times.

Abarth modifies Fiat engines in any number of different ways, even adding double overhead camshafts. As a result, Fiat-Abarths run in a number of different SCCA classes. The same is true of Abarth's cars built around the Simca engine. Here's an abbreviated rundown on several Abarth cars:

Fiat-Abarth 850/S Record Monza	847 cc. OHV	57 bhp.
Fiat-Abarth 700 Twin Cam	695 cc. DOHC	65 bhp.
Fiat-Abarth 750 Twin Cam	748 cc. DOHC	70 bhp.
Fiat-Abarth 1000 Twin Cam	995 cc. DOHC	105 bhp.
Simca-Abarth 2000	1946 cc. DOHC	202 bhp.
Simca-Abarth 1300	1288 cc. DOHC	138 bhp.

FORD (American)

FORD GT

Engine: V-8 OHV	4728 cc.	385 bhp.
1825 pounds	0–60: 5 secs. (est.)	Max. speed: 200 mph.

Ford's GT represents the first all-out attempt at international sports car laurels by a major American manufacturer in several decades. In 1964 and 1965, its successes were less than overwhelming. But a 1965 class win at Sebring and an over-all victory at Daytona proved that, despite dismal showings in Europe, the car had plenty of promise.

In every respect but one, the Fiberglas-bodied Ford GT is the very model of the modern GT car. Rear-mounted engine, 5-speed gearbox, fully independent suspension, disc brakes all around, and a gorgeously aerodynamic two-seater coupe body are the earmarks of such a car. The Ford has them all.

It's her engine that's different. It's not the sophisticated overhead-cam racing jewel of a Porsche or a Ferrari . . . but rather a hopped-up version of the 289 cu. inch pushrod V-8 that's powered many a production line Ford, Fairlane and Mustang. But where the hottest of these engines produced some 270 horsepower, the GT's 289 delivers over 40 per cent more. Four twin-throat Weber carburetors are part of the reason, along with the most careful kind of tuning, balancing, polishing, and assembly. Several 427 cu. inch, 500 bhp. Ford V-8's have also been dropped into Ford GT's, with amazing results.

Ford GT coupe with 289 cu. in. engine shows its speed at Le Mans.

The Ford GT design is the result of a three-way collaboration of Eric Broadley (the Lola's designer), Roy Lunn (first of British Ford and now of U.S.), and John Wyer, formerly of Aston Martin. In mid-1965, Ford started the construction of fifty coupes (to qualify for a specific GT class) and the development and sale of these vehicles ($16,250 per copy) was assigned to Carroll Shelby of Cobra and Mustang fame. They could hardly be in better hands.

Roadster version of Ford GT has faired-in roll bar behind seat.

JAGUAR (British)

JAGUAR XK 150S

	Engine: 6 cyl. DOHC	3781 cc.	265 bhp.
3200 pounds	0–60: 7½ secs.		Max. speed: 135 mph.

The XK 150S was the last in a series of production Jaguar sports cars whose first model, the XK 120, appeared in 1948. Bred from the XK 120 were the XK 120M, XK 120MC, XK 140, XK 140MC, XK 150, and finally, the XK 150S. Throughout the whole line, Jaguar's policy has been one of evolutionary development, rather than one of radical redesign. (The output of the DOHC XK engine grew, model by model, from 160 bhp. to 265 bhp.—a 66 per cent increase in power, on an increase in size of only 10 per cent!) Many of the features incorporated in the series are those developed in European competition on the firm's racing sports cars. Typical are the four-wheel disc brakes on the XK 150S—a feature the company proved on its Le Mans-winning D-type.

The XK 150S shows its heritage in its lines and character—those of a relatively big, relatively heavy, very powerful car. It is distinguishable from earlier XK's by its wider, more sloping lines, and by its larger grille. One of the car's greatest charms is its true dual-purpose character—it can be raced and toured with equal ease. Leather seats and roll-up windows exemplify the touring luxury of this car.

An earlier model of the XK 150S was equipped with a 3.4 liter engine of 250 bhp., but otherwise is almost identical with the 3.8 car.

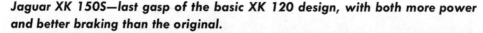

Jaguar XK 150S—last gasp of the basic XK 120 design, with both more power and better braking than the original.

XK-E styling is in complete contrast with Jaguar tradition.

JAGUAR XK-E

Engine: 6 cyl. DOHC	4235 cc.	265 bhp.
2700 pounds	0–60: 7 secs.	Max. speed: 150 mph.

Unquestionably, the XK-E is the most sensational production Jaguar since the XK 120. For this car, with a single leap, brings Jaguar up-to-date with the Sixties. Gone are 500 pounds, the live rear axle, and the slightly dowdy look of the XK 150S. In their place is fully independent rear suspension and a sleek steel body that's less than four feet high at the top of the windshield!

And yet, with typical good sense, Jaguar has retained the durable DOHC 6-cyl. engine. Although while far from modern in design (it's still close to the one that powered the XK 120 of 1948), its sturdiness made it a most logical choice for the new car. Disc brakes (what else on a Jaguar?) are mounted at the wheels in front, next to the differential at the rear. Torsion bars take care of springing in front, coil springs in the back. Even the 4-speed gearbox is new in the 4.2 liter XK-E . . . a good thing, since the boxes fitted to the earlier 3.8 liter XK-E's had a reputation for something less than perfect speed and smoothness.

The XK-E has not chalked up an impressive record in U.S. competition. But time, tuning (and perhaps an aluminum body) may help.

Lola T-70: A far cry from the 1100 cc. cars that made Lola famous.

LOLA (British)

LOLA TYPE 70

Engine: V-8 OHV (Ford)	4728 cc.	375 bhp. (app.)
1375 pounds	0–60: 5 secs. (est.)	Max. speed: 180 mph. (est.)

Lola's first entry on the American scene was a remarkably successful front-engined G Modified machine. Powered by the ubiquitous 1100 cc. Coventry-Climax engine, this 825-pound car racked up eleven wins in eleven races in her debutante year, 1959.

Since that time, Lola's designer has turned his hand to Formula Jr., Formula I, and in 1963, to a GT coupe which was to evolve into the Ford GT. The Ford bears a number of resemblances to the Lola 70.

The Lola is Broadley's approach to the big-bore sports racing car problem. Its chassis is a semi-monocoque structure of welded and riveted steel and aluminum. The engine compartment can hold any of several big American V-8's—the Ford 289, modified Chevrolet 327, or you name it. A 4-speed Hewland or a 5-speed ZF gearbox gets the power to the wheels. Suspension is fully independent, and all four brakes are disc. Beneath the Fiberglas body, a 30-gallon aluminum gas tank lies at each side of the driver. With the Chevy engine, side-draft Weber carburetors are used; down-draft Webers feed the Ford.

For a car that is only 31″ high, this new Lola stands very tall in racing. Until 4-wheel drive arrives, this type of design should be just about the last word.

LOTUS (British)

LOTUS SUPER SEVEN

Engine: 4 cyl. OHV	1498 cc.	96 bhp.
1050 pounds	0–60: 8 secs.	Max. speed: 115 mph.

A combination of light weight, reliable power, and outstanding handling make this Lotus a no-holds-barred contender. Her push-rod engine is derived from the British Ford 116E. Modifications by master English tuner Cosworth include a new camshaft, work on the head, and 2 double-throat Weber carburetors. 4-speed gearbox is also English Ford. Many of her other components come from production cars, including the live rear axle. Disc brakes are up front, drums at the rear. Despite the apparently unsophisticated design, handling is the Super Seven's long suit. Weight distribution is right on the classic 50/50 target.

A less potent version of the Seven comes equipped with 1340 cc. Cosworth-Ford engine. And apparently identical Lotuses race in the lower classes when powered by 1 liter Ford or BMC engines.

Original English motorcycle front fenders of Lotus Super Seven are replaced by faired fenders to meet American regulations.

Tiny Lotus Elan can hang right in there with XK-E's, Corvettes.

LOTUS ELAN

Engine: 4 cyl. DOHC   1558 cc.   145 bhp.

1475 pounds   0–60: 7 secs.   Max. speed: 130 mph.

This tiny bomb stands less than four feet tall, is 15″ shorter than a Volkswagen. Yet its fantastic performance makes it competitive with even some Corvettes and Ferraris.

Lotus boss Colin Chapman is seldom bound by traditions—even his own. For the Elan, he came up with a totally new steel-box backbone—a sort of elongated "X" with the engine resting between the front legs, the differential between the rear. For despite the trend to rear engines, the Elan's is up front.

It's quite an engine. The block and bottom are English Ford-based. But the top is a twin-cam head designed and developed by Lotus. Two twin-choke Weber carburetors are used. Transmission is 4-speed, and also by Ford.

Suspension is fully independent, and the Elan's handling proves that it's one of the best in the world. Four-wheel disc brakes stop the car. Body is Fiberglas, with retractable headlamps for aerodynamic smoothness.

In 1965, the Elan was classed by the SCCA with such potent machinery as the Porsche Carrera 1600 and Alfa Romeo GTZ. If there was any doubt about the Elan's prowess at the beginning of the season, there was none at the end. Elans were class champs in four out of five SCCA divisions.

Lotus Elite Coupé. Right-hand British drive is ideal for clockwise circuits.

LOTUS ELITE (Stage III)   CLASS C PRODUCTION
    Engine: 4 cyl. SOHC   1216 cc.   100 bhp.
1450 pounds (dry)   0–60: 9 secs.   Max. speed: 130 mph.

The Elite was an earlier Lotus entry into the dual-purpose sports car field. Her performance is remarkable, and is due largely to her unusually light weight. For comparison, she's only 300 pounds heavier than the Porsche RSK, an all-out competition car.

The Elite owes most of her light weight to radical body construction. She has integral body-frame construction, but the material used is largely fiberglass, with a bare minimum of steel reinforcement. No other car could make that statement in the late 1950's.

The engine that powers the Elite is a bored-out Coventry Climax unit of the type that's used in the Lotus 1100 cc. sports racing cars. It's detuned a bit, for less power but more tractability and reliability. Disc brakes on all four wheels, plus fully independent rear suspension complete one of the most up-to-date little packages on road or track.

A somewhat less potent version of the Elite was also available. This one is powered by a less highly-tuned Climax engine which turns out approximately 75 bhp.

Lotus 23 is a most popular car in small-bore modified racing, may be powered by Ford, Climax, BMC, Alfa, or even Porsche engine.

LOTUS TWENTY-THREE

Engine: 4-cyl. OHV   1498 cc.   125 bhp.

950 pounds   0–60: 6 secs. (app.)   Max. speed: 145 mph. (app.)

Sometimes a single car can make a whole class. Such was the case with the Twenty-three's illustrious grandparent, the Eleven. In the middle and late fifties, the Eleven dominated G Modified (1100 cc.) racing. Challenged by the newer Lolas and Elvas, Colin Chapman moved on to the Lotus Seventeen. And then, in 1962, he came up with the Lotus 23— one of his most successful and long-lived designs.

The Twenty-three may be fitted with any number of small- or middle-sized engines. For G Modified racing, the Cosworth-Ford 1100 cc. 100 bhp. engine or the Climax 1150 cc. SOHC are the most likely choices. For F Modified racing, it'll be a pushrod 125 bhp. 1500 cc. Cosworth Ford. Or the 1600 cc. DOHC Lotus-Ford of approximately 150 bhp. Private owners may fit other engines (Alfas, for example), or, as in the 1965 USRRC championship car, Porsches.

The Twenty-three has a tubular steel space frame under her Fiberglas body. Oil and water travel from rear-mounted engine to front-mounted radiators right through the tubes of the frame. Suspension is fully independent, with disc brakes all around. 4- or 5-speed gearboxes are used, of Renault or VW derivation.

LOTUS THIRTY

Engine: V-8 OHV (Ford)	4728 cc.	350 bhp.
1350 pounds	0–60: 5 secs. (est.)	Max. speed: 190 mph.

Just about every race car designer has had a crack at mating a big American V-8 with a ultra-light chassis. Often it has resulted in shoe-horning a Ford or Chevy into a chassis originally designed to take a much smaller engine. But the Lotus Thirty was an all-new design—strictly for American V-8's.

Backbone of the Thirty is a central steel box frame. Into the center section of this box are crammed water and oil pipes, hydraulic lines, control cables and wiring, plus a flexible rubber fuel tank. (More fuel is contained in the box sections which run beneath each door.) The rear-mounted and much-modified pushrod Ford 289 is equipped with either downdraft Weber carburetors or fuel injection. A five-speed German ZF transmission lies behind the engine.

The one-piece Fiberglas body is less than three feet tall at its highest point. Suspension is fully independent, and disc brakes are used.

Though often successful, the Thirty suffered from numerous teething troubles. In 1965, it was superseded by the Lotus Forty; powered by a 350 cu. inch version of the Ford V-8 which puts out well over 400 bhp.

Colin Chapman builds a car for American V-8's, calls it the Lotus 30.

MG (British)

Many an American driver—Phil Hill, Carroll Shelby, and John Fitch, to name but a famous few—cut his sports car racing teeth on an MG. Though seldom seen in current racing, the classic MG-TC, -TD, and -TF's gave millions of Americans their first look at a really available sports car. For the record, here's how these MG's stacked up:

Model	Displace.	Hp.	Engine	Wgt.	0–60	Max. speed
TC (1948)	1250 cc.	54 bhp.	4 cyl. OHV	1850 lbs.	22 secs.	75 mph.
TD (1950)	1250 cc.	54 bhp.	4 cyl. OHV	2000 lbs.	20 secs.	80 mph.
TF (1954)	1250 cc.	57 bhp.	4 cyl. OHV	2000 lbs.	19 secs.	80 mph.
TF (1955)	1500 cc.	65 bhp.	4 cyl. OHV	2000 lbs.	16 secs.	85 mph.

MGA 1600 Mark II

Engine: 4 cyl. OHV   1622 cc.   90 bhp.

2000 pounds   0–60: 12½ secs.   Max. speed: 105 mph.

In 1956, MG introduced the first of a new line, the MGA's. The first had a 1500 cc., 72 bhp. engine, and could almost touch 100 mph. The more powerful MGA 1600 with front disc brakes followed it in 1959. Latest was the 1600 Mark II. All MGA's are sturdy, "forgiving" cars, and unlike the postwar T Series, are handsomely streamlined.

MG's 1958 attempt at a car with a DOHC conversion of the MGA engine (the MGA Twin Cam) is also no longer in production. The DOHC engine was powerful, but proved sadly fragile in competition.

Close battle is typical of MGA competition.

For racing in GT category, MGB can be fitted with hardtop.

MGB

Engine: 4 cyl. OHV	1798 cc.	98 bhp.
2050 pounds	0–60: 11 secs.	Max. speed: 110 mph.

In 1962, a new MG hit the road: the MGB. Mechanically, it held no surprises, but continued an MG tradition started in the postwar Forties. But a new steel body now covers the typically British innards—and a very good-looking one it is.

Under the hood is a slightly larger (11 per cent) engine than that which powered the MGA. Though horsepower is only slightly increased, the bigger engine delivers more torque, and hence better acceleration. The bigger engine responds better to tuning than did the MGA's—under 1966 SCCA rules, for example, close to 140 bhp. could be squeezed from it.

From the engine on back, the car is also very much MG. There's a four-speed transmission, with synchromesh on the top three gears. And at the back is British Motor Corporation's beloved old live axle, with drum brakes out at its ends. Up front, of course, are discs.

The car is a solid, very reliable performer—easy to drive and easy to maintain. Priced at well under $3000, it's a remarkable buy. And even giving away almost half a liter to the TR-4's, it can still whip them on occasion.

Mercedes 300SL roadster at full tilt.

MERCEDES-BENZ (German)

MERCEDES-BENZ 300SL

Engine: 6 cyl. SOHC, fuel-injected	2996 cc.	240 bhp.
3000 pounds	0–60: 7 secs.	Max. speed: 150 mph.

Product of a glorious racing background that stretches back dozens of years, the 300SL shows every bit of its breeding. The famous gull-wing coupe (now no longer in production) was the first postwar Mercedes to make a mark in American sports car racing.

The 300SL roadster followed the coupe. It is slightly more powerful, but also slightly heavier. Obviously it is one of the world's most beautiful cars, though perhaps not as sleek as the coupe.

Mechanically the 300SL has a number of interesting features. With the Corvette it shares the distinction of using fuel injection rather than multiple carburetion. The 300SL's rear axle is a special Mercedes design of swing axle called the "low-pivot" rear axle. It employs coil springs at each rear wheel, and a third coil spring between the two wheels to control their interaction. To keep the hood line of the car low, Mercedes designers have tilted the water-cooled engine at a forty-degree angle. (Chrysler's Valiant cants its engine for the same reason.) The frame is tubular steel. Drum brakes are fitted.

Uncompromising look marks the Mor
This one carries disc brakes.

MORGAN (British)

MORGAN PLUS FOUR

Engine: 4 cyl. OHV (Triumph)	2138 cc.	105 bhp.
1940 pounds	0–60: 11 secs.	Max. speed: 105 mph.

The way a man takes to the looks of a Morgan is a fair guide to his ideas about automobiles. Today, Morgan is a lonely reminder of "traditional" British sports car styling. To some it may be ugly and raw-boned, but to most enthusiasts it is rather nostalgically "right."

Looks aside, the Plus Four is quite an impressive performer. No match for the Triumph whose engine she carries, she's still a powerful, rugged automobile. A live rear axle handicaps her road-holding, but together with a stiff suspension and a supple wooden frame, it's an ingratiating reminder of an older day. Morgan enthusiasts are a very dedicated bunch.

A hotter Morgan—the Super Sport—is also available. She boasts two Weber carburetors and an aluminum body that's lighter than the Plus Four's. And there's a Morgan with 1.5 liter Ford engine—not as powerful as the Plus Four, but almost as much fun.

PORSCHE (German)

PORSCHE 1600 SC

| | Engine: 4 cyl. opposed, OHV | 1582 cc. | 95 bhp. |

2000 pounds (coupe)   0–60: 12 secs.   Max. speed: 115 mph.

Porsches have chalked up a fantastic record in American racing. Both pushrod-engined cars and Carreras have won victory after victory, while in modified racing, the RS Porsches long held sway.

All these marvels bear the name of Dr. Ferdinand Porsche, great German designer of such famous cars as the Auto-Union Grand Prix monsters of pre-World War II days, the Volkswagen, and a revolutionary Formula I car called the Cisitalia. Porsche died in 1951, and the Stuttgart firm today is run by his son, Ferry Porsche.

Until the coming of the SOHC 911 in 1965, production Porsches had pushrod engines like that of the 1600 SC. The engines appeared in 1300, 1500, and 1600 versions, the most powerful of which was that in the 1600 SC (95 German horsepower, 107 SAE). Porsche "trademarks" incorporated in the SC are air-cooling, rear engine, horizontally opposed four cylinders, independent four-wheel suspension, swing axle, torsion bars instead of springs, and "chassis-less" steel body.

Porsche Super—in the now continued Speedster body.

The Carrera GT looks just about like any other Porsche—until you lift the rear deck and see the DOHC engine.

PORSCHE CARRERA 2000

Engine: 4 cyl. opposed, DOHC (2)   1966 cc.   180 bhp.

2000 pounds (coupe)   0–60: 8 secs.   Max. speed: 140 mph.
1800 pounds (Speedster)

Tucked underneath the touring bodywork of the Porsche Carreras were slightly detuned versions of the Porsche 4-cylinder double-overhead-camshaft racing engines. The more recent versions of this potent car were powered by a 2-liter engine, earlier models by 1500 or 1600 cc. engines. Neither car is now in production. The Carrera may appear as a roadster, a convertible, or a coupe. (The roadster, or "Speedster," is lightest, and hence more desirable for most racing.)

The DOHC racing engine is classic Porsche: opposed four cylinders, air-cooled. Its greater output is due primarily to the use of the twin cams, but of course increased carburetion and compression are necessary to make full use of the DOHC potential.

Despite being classed as a production car by the SCCA, the Carrera is a noisy, fussy racing car—extremely effective in its class.

Porsche Spider was longtime champ of under 1600 cc. racing.

PORSCHE 1500 RSK SPIDER   CLASS F MODIFIED

Engine: 4 cyl. opposed, DOHC (2)   1498 cc.   160 bhp.

1150   Max. speed:
pounds (dry)   0–60: not available, probably around 6 secs.   160 mph.

Unquestionably, the RSK was one of the most successful of small modified sports cars—with an astounding string of both European and American victories. It was powered by the hottest versions of the DOHC Porsche engine in all its displacements: 1500 cc., 1600 cc., 1700 cc., and 2000 cc., ranging from 160 bhp. to almost 200 bhp.

The RSK differed from the production Porsches of its day in several interesting ways. The engine is *ahead* of the rear axle, not behind it. Rear suspension consisted of a low-pivot swing axle, wishbones, and coil springs. And the flyweight light-alloy body was hung on a frame built up of welded tubing. Body and frame were not integral.

Beginning in 1960, the sports-racing Porsches were given new designations whose digits referred to the year of the car's construction. These cars—RS-60, RS-61, etc., followed the RSK's design.

Porsche 904. Under the bobtailed body, a traditional Porsche engine.

PORSCHE 904

Engine: 4 cyl. opposed, DOHC (2)   1966 cc.   180 bhp.

1350 pounds   0–60: 5.5 secs.   Max. speed: 160 mph.

This is a production car? Well, the SCCA says so—which simply means that enough have been built to make it so by the rule book. But everything about the 904 itself says "racer"—despite the fact that you can buy a detuned version for street use. *If* you've got $8000.

Frame of the Porsche 904 consists of two boxy steel side members, to which the Fiberglas body is directly bonded. The whole tail lifts off for access to the engine. The engine is the tried-and-true DOHC Porsche racing four, air-cooled as usual. Fully independent suspension is by triangular arms and coil springs, front and back. A 5-speed gearbox gets the 904 moving, disc brakes pull it to a stop. To keep pit stops to a minimum, a 30-gallon fuel tank is under the hood.

Really too slow to play tag with the Cobras, the 904 is peculiarly classed for American amateur racing. But as a GT car in USRRC or international events, it's nothing short of sensational.

Shelby's Ford Cobra challenged Europe's best; beat them hands down.

SHELBY AMERICAN (American)

COBRA 427

| Engine: V-8 OHV (Ford) | 6997 cc. | 485 bhp. |
| 2350 pounds | 0–60: 4.5 secs. | Max. speed: 175 mph. |

Squeezing big American V-8's into imported chassis has long been a popular pastime with backyard "special" builders. More often than not, the results have been jerry-built rigs that handled badly and broke up frequently. But Shelby American is no backyard builder—as the myriad racing successes of their Cobras amply prove.

Shelby American is largely Carroll Shelby, champion American driver, now retired from racing. It was Shelby who, in 1962, approached AC Cars of England with the idea of dropping a Ford V-8 into their AC Ace two-seater. It was only a 260 cu. inch Ford then—but it added up to a 140 mph. automobile—more car than AC had ever been able to deliver using British Ford or Bristol engines.

Now . . . would the Bristol chassis handle a Ford 289 cu. inch engine? It would, and it did. Not without some beefing up, but that was done, and done well. With as much as 345 horsepower to shove around not much more than 2000 pounds of automobile, the 289 Cobra was a fantastic performer. It gave fits to Sting Rays, Ferraris, and just about everything else that tried to get in its way.

In the search for even more power, an entirely different engine was pressed into service: the big 427 cu. inch Ford—prepared and tuned as it is for NASCAR stock car racing. And with it, the Cobra became even more formidable.

Between them, the 289 and 427 Cobras have chalked up a remarkable record. Almost complete domination of the SCCA's top production class in 1963, 1964, and 1965. Winners of the Manufacturer's Championship in the USRRC series for three years running ('63 to '65). Things didn't go too badly in international competition, either. In 1965, the Cobras captured the FIA World GT Manufacturer's Championship, too— absolutely clobbering, of all things, the Ferraris.

In basic design, the 289 Cobra and the 427 are much the same. Most striking difference between the two is in suspension. Both cars have independent rear suspension. But where the 289 depended on a transverse leaf spring and lower A-arms, the 427 uses upper and lower A-arms with coil springing.

Otherwise, the two cars are similar in design. One or two four-barrel carburetors feed the big front-mounted V-8's. (In FIA competition, Webers may be fitted.) An American 4-speed transmission backs up the engine. A simple ladder-type tubular steel frame is used, with lighter steel tubes above it carrying the aluminum body. Brakes are discs at all four wheels.

MUSTANG 350 GT (COMPETITION VERSION)

Engine: V-8 OHV	4727 cc.	345 bhp.
2550 pounds	0–60: 5.5 secs.	Max. speed: 145 mph.

Maybe it looks like a Mustang—but it sure doesn't act like one. Horsepower is up, weight is down. And road-holding and braking are vastly improved over the standard production Mustang. The result is a snarling, spitting, competition fastback that was designed to dominate one whole SCCA production class. In its first year in competition, it did just that.

GT 350 looks like a Mustang, but doesn't act like one.

Up front in the 350 GT is a high-performance version of the Ford 289 V-8, boosted from 271 horsepower to 345 with the help of such modifications as a special aluminum manifold, special four-barrel carburetion, and a free-flowing exhaust system that's almost wholly unmuffled. A large capacity aluminum sump holds oil, and an oil-cooler is added as well. Big disc brakes stop the front wheels, and metallic-lined drums are at the rear. A heavy-duty four-speed gearbox is standard equipment, as is a limited-slip differential.

Road-holding of the 350 GT is improved by detail changes in the front suspension, and by more radical rear suspension alterations. The rear axle is still Ford and still "live," but its movements are far more positively controlled in the competition car. Bigger wheels (magnesium) and bigger tires (racing Goodyears) put more rubber on the road than do the standard Mustang's.

And if that weren't enough, the 350 GT is a lot lighter than the garden-variety Mustang—about 400 pounds. A number of items account for this: Fiberglas hood and front apron, plastic side and rear windows, lighter seats, and aluminum in places like the sump and transmission case.

There's a "street version" of the Mustang 350 GT too—with a little bit less of almost everything described above.

SUNBEAM (British)

SUNBEAM ALPINE IV

Engine: 4 cyl. OHV   1592 cc.   88 bhp.

2200 pounds   0–60: 14 secs.   Max. speed: 100 mph.

Underneath the unquestionably modern body of the Alpine lies a car which is typically British. The OHV engine, the front (only) disc brakes, and the live rear axle are all marks of good traditional British design. Together they add up to a two-seater that's a comfortable touring car . . . and no slouch on the track.

The Alpine faces some pretty respectable opponents in her class. But she can be a good match for most of them. In the Alpine's first three years in America, for example, one never failed to finish among the top three in class in SCCA national point standings.

In a higher SCCA class, you'll often see an Alpine that doesn't act like one at all. This is the Sunbeam Tiger—same body, but with an American Ford V-8 tucked under her bonnet. Since the Ford puts out well over twice the horsepower of the Sunbeam engine, it makes a pretty startling change in the car's performance (a top speed of over 130 mph., for example). Rear disc brakes and a Ford gearbox are added to handle the extra power.

Sunbeam Alpine: a good-looker that's made good in racing.

Triumph Spitfire boasts independent rear suspension, lively performance.

TRIUMPH (British)

TRIUMPH SPITFIRE MARK II

Engine: 4 cyl. OHV	1147 cc.	67 bhp.
1625 pounds	0–60: 15 secs.	Max. speed: 95 mph.

Like the MGB and the Austin Healey 3000, the Triumph TR-4 also has a kid sister. She's the Triumph Spitfire, introduced in 1962 and updated a bit with the appearance of the Mark II in 1965.

The Spitfire is quite a sophisticated little piece of machinery—particularly considering her British origins. Based on the Triumph Herald, she has fully independent rear suspension: quite a rarity in a low-priced (about $2200) sports car.

Powering the Spitfire is a water-cooled engine that has proved remarkably reliable under racing stresses—and made the car very competitive in its class. Two SU carburetors are used. (With modifications, including Weber carburetion, as much as 105 bhp. can be extracted from these same four cylinders.) Behind the engine is a 4-speed gearbox, with synchromesh on the top three speeds. Disc brakes are used on the front only. Covering all with good looks is an all-steel body—designed, like the TR-4's, by Michelotti.

A TR-4 stripped for the course . . . bumpers off, windshield replaced with small windscreen. Cockpit cover lowers wind resistance.

TRIUMPH TR-4

Engine: 4 cyl. OHV	2183 cc.	105 bhp.
2250 pounds	0–60: 11 secs.	Max speed: 110 mph.

The TR-4 is the latest in a Triumph line that stretches back to 1952. Model by model, a really excellent car has been developed.

Differences between the TR-4 and its immediate predecessor are slight in all but one respect: body work. While the TR-3 carried a somewhat lumpy, bug-eyed body, the newer car is dressed in a crisper and far more appealing one by the Italian Michelotti. Wind-up windows, a large (by sports car standards) trunk, and optional rear jump seats make the car as attractive for town as for track.

Engine refinements (principally bigger-bored cylinder liners for an extra 150 cc.) give the TR-4 a 5 bhp. edge on the TR-3. These liners may, however, be installed in a TR-3 engine for SCCA competition. Like the TR-3, the TR-4 has 4-speed gearbox, live rear axle, and front disc brakes. In 1965, the TR4A arrived: essentially a TR-4, but with optional independent rear suspension and much-improved road-holding.

The Turner—simple, lively, effective.

TURNER (British)

TURNER 950 SPORTS

| Engine: 4 cyl. OHV | 948 cc. | 61 bhp. |
| 1250 pounds | 0–60: 14 secs. | Max. speed: 90 mph. |

Like the Austin-Healey Sprite, the Turner is powered by a modified BMC Type A engine. But greater modifications—among them a more efficient cylinder head and a higher compression ratio—make the engine 10 per cent more powerful than the Sprite's.

Austin parts are used liberally in the suspensions of both cars. But where the Sprite uses quarter-elliptic rear springs, the Turner employs torsion bars. Biggest difference is the body material. The Sprite's is steel, while the Turner's is fiberglass. The stock Turner brakes are drum, but front disc brakes are an approved option. The transmission and differential hold no surprises. Four forward speeds and a live rear axle are typical in a car of this price, size, and nationality.

Finally, the Turner may also be fitted with the famous 1100 cc. SOHC Coventry-Climax engine. Or a Weber-carbureted 1500 cc. Ford engine. Both race in higher classes than the BMC-engined Turner.

Rugged Volvo P1800 wasn't really built for racing, but proved good at it anyway.

VOLVO (Swedish)

VOLVO P1800

Engine: 4 cyl. OHV	1778 cc.	108 bhp.
2450 pounds	0–60: 13.5 secs.	Max. speed: 110 mph.

You won't see a lot of P1800's on the track—but the ones that do race usually do pretty well. And that's a little surprising—because this car was designed strictly as a Grand Touring car—not as a racer. You can buy a lot more pure performance for $4000—but hardly more touring comfort.

Still, the Volvo has a lot going for it. Sheer ruggedness, for one thing. The 5 main bearing engine has a great reputation for reliability, and is so understressed that a lot of extra power can be coaxed out of it without damaging a thing. Sturdiness is evident in every component, all the way back to the "live" rear axle. There's a hefty 4-speed gearbox—plus overdrive. And good disc brakes up front, with rear discs available as an optional extra.

Against the Volvo is its weight. 2450 pounds is a lot of fat for a little over 100 bhp. to push around. Excess weight may not hurt a touring car much, but in racing, where acceleration is crucial, it's a mighty drawback. Still, reliability is not to be sniffed at. Volvos are often running long after more fragile machinery has come unstuck.

A PORTFOLIO OF
RACING PHOTOS

THE COURSES

Recent years have seen the almost complete disappearance of racing on U.S. public roads. Such road-racing, with its incalculable dangers to driver and spectator alike, has had its colorful day in this country. And while the passing of open road-racing may be lamented by some, it is clear to most that the sport has literally outgrown it. Surely few who love the sport would wish to see such racing reborn. Almost every mishap on an open road course is followed by a flock of restrictive—sometimes oppressive—laws and ordinances. American racing today is on the airport course and the closed road course . . . where it belongs.

Unfortunately the airport course is a poor substitute for a road course. It is relatively dull for the driver. It has no uphill or downhill sections, no tricky camber. And it is less than ideal for the spectator, too. Unless spectators can use grandstands or other raised viewing points, its flatness limits the spectator's view.

Historically, as mentioned in Chapter 1, the airport course played an important role. It served as an interim scene of action between the colorful but dangerous open road course, and the inestimably safer (and scarcely less colorful) closed road course. The airport course offers safety and good crowd control. In areas where crowds are too small to make investment in a closed road course profitable, the airport course will undoubtedly continue to serve. But it seems likely that as more and more road courses are built, the use of airports as simulated road courses will gradually vanish into the past.

The existence of more than thirty closed road courses in the U.S. (and the yearly reports of new ones a-building) is a sure sign that sports car racing is here to stay. Like the modern ski area, the closed road course is expensive to build. It is inevitably a risky business proposition, sometimes a downright ruinous one. Simply putting together enough reasonably priced acreage in an area that's suitably close to a good source of spectators is an extraordinarily arduous, time- and money-consuming job. And even after the course has been built— the money invested, the earth moved and paved—local laws and local opposition can plague a course severely. Everyone who loves motor sport owes much to the enthusiasts and entrepreneurs who have built America's closed road courses. Long may they reap their dividends, both sporting and financial.

To the driver the closed road course offers every challenge (barring only two-way traffic and pedestrians!) of the open road. Yet most road courses—and all of the best ones—also offer him a considerable degree of safety. There are escape roads, sand banks, permanent and reliable communications systems, and almost perfect crowd control. The driver can keep his mind on driving fast and skillfully. Should his speed exceed his skill, there's room for him to recover himself.

For the spectator the closed road course is equally advantageous. For one thing, he can *see*. Hillsides and rises of land provide natural grandstands, often supplemented by man-made ones. At many courses the spectator can drive his car around, *inside* the circuit, from one vantage point to another. Usually he can buy his lunch without standing in line for a lifetime, and even send his wife off to the ladies' room knowing that it's in better shape than a hillbilly privy.

But most important, the closed road course is *safe* for the spectator. There are many very good and many very eloquent arguments for the proposition that a competitor who has chosen to risk his life may do so. But there are far fewer why unsuspecting spectators should be exposed to danger. Spectator injuries are almost unknown on the closed road course. If they do occur—as once in a long while they may—it is almost invariably because some spectator has strayed to a spot where the merest shred of good sense would have told him he shouldn't be.

On the following pages are profiles of twenty-one American courses. Most of the facts recorded about them speak for themselves. But a few deserve a little commentary;

SPECTATOR AREAS: The recommended areas are those that the authors personally like, or that tend to attract a considerable proportion of the crowd. Do not take the authors' or the crowd's preferences for gospel; just for guidance.

LAP RECORD: If you compare the lap records for several courses, you will soon get an idea of which courses are "fast" and which are "slow." Both types are equally exciting . . . although in different ways. Where lap records set by cars over 1600 cc. are close to those set by cars under 1600 or 2000 cc., there is always a chance of enjoying one of the very best of all closely contested battles, the little-car/big-car duel.

RESTRICTIONS: Don't overlook these. Sometimes you can save yourself a long, fruitless drive if it's raining.

SANCTION: These are the organizations that sanction or approve racing on the course.

ANNUAL EVENTS: Dates and events are always tentative. Events may change from year to year—both their location and their date. For most courses phone numbers are given as well as addresses (in the Information section). Phone or write first and be sure there's going to *be* a race.

Unfortunately, this book is short, and the list of American courses is long. Here are the locations of some of the courses that could *not* be covered in these pages:

ALABAMA
   Decatur (Courtland—25 mi. W. of Decatur Airport)
ARIZONA
   Tucson (Municipal Airport)
   Phoenix (Phoenix International Raceway)
CALIFORNIA
   Los Angeles (County Fairgrounds, Pomona)
   Los Angeles (Willow Springs Raceways—50 mi. N. of Los Angeles)
   Oakland (International Airport)
   Sacramento (Vaca Valley, Vacaville—40 mi. SW. of Sacramento)
   San Diego (Fairgrounds, Del Mar—15 mi. N. of San Diego)
   San Francisco (Candlestick Park)
   San Francisco (Cotati—50 mi. N. of San Francisco)

COLORADO
  Aspen (Aspen Raceways)
FLORIDA
  North Palm Beach (Palm Beach International Raceway)
GEORGIA
  Augusta (Augusta International Speedway)
  Bainbridge (Dixie Raceways)
  Donalsonville (Airport)
  Savannah (Savannah-Effingham Motorway)
INDIANA
  Indianapolis (Indianapolis Raceway Park, Clermont)
IOWA
  Des Moines (Greenwood Roadway, Indianola)
KANSAS
  Garden City (road course)
LOUISIANA
  New Orleans (Hammond, airport—60 mi. NW. of New Orleans)
  Shreveport (DeSoto Airport, Mansfield—40 mi. S. of Shreveport)
  Shreveport (Louisiana Hilltop Raceway, Bossier City)
MICHIGAN
  Detroit (Waterford Hills—20 mi. N. of Detroit)
  Grand Rapids (Kent Field)
  Saginaw (Grayling—115 mi. N. of Saginaw)
MINNESOTA
  Bloomington (Metropolitan Stadium)
MISSOURI
  St. Louis (Mid-America Raceways, Wentzville—45 mi. W. of St. Louis)
NEBRASKA
  Alliance (Airfield)
NEW HAMPSHIRE
  Concord (Bryar Motorsport Park, London—10 mi. N. of Concord)
NEW JERSEY
  Vineland (Vineland Speedway—35 mi. S. of Philadelphia)
NEW YORK
  Buffalo (Dunkirk Airport, 50 mi. SW. of Buffalo)
OHIO
  Warren (Nelson Ledges—10 mi. W. of Warren)
OKLAHOMA
  Enid (Vance Air Force Base)
  Ponca City (road course)

OREGON
> *Goshen* (Oregon International Raceway—6 mi. S. of Eugene)

PENNSYLVANIA
> *Connellsville* (Airport—30 mi. SE. of Pittsburgh)
> *Long Pond* (Pocono International Raceway)
> *Reading* (Municipal Airport)
> *Wilkes-Barre* (Giant's Despair Hillclimb, Berwick)

SOUTH CAROLINA
> *Spartanburg* (Airport)

TEXAS
> *Galveston* (Scholes Field)
> *Midland* (Rattlesnake Raceway—the Chaparral's test track)
> *Houston*
> *Smithfield* (Green Valley road course)

UTAH
> *Salt Lake City* (West Jordan)

VERMONT
> *Manchester* (Mount Equinox Hillclimb)

WASHINGTON
> *Tacoma* (Shelton, airport—50 mi. W. of Tacoma)

WISCONSIN
> *Milwaukee* (Lynndale Farms, Pewaukee—20 mi. W. of Milwaukee)
> *Milwaukee* (Milwaukee Fairgrounds, West Allis)
> *Wilmot* (Wilmot Hills—midway between Chicago and Milwaukee)

And now for the profiles of the twenty-one. All of the most important American courses are included, as well as a few that are interesting by virtue of their location or the fact that at least one major race is run on them each year. Any of them—all of them—are well worth more than a single visit.

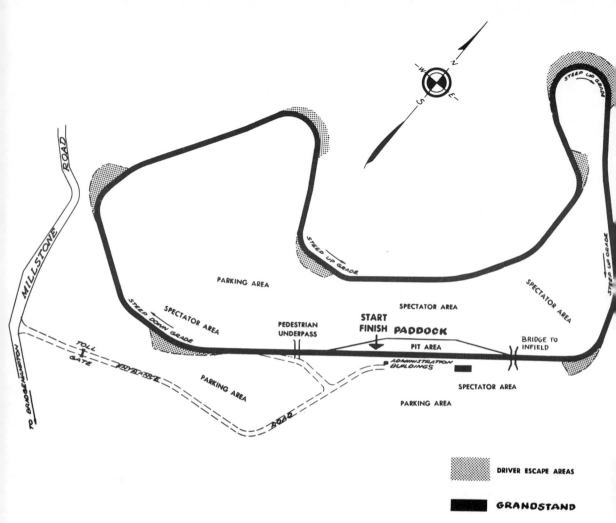

BRIDGEHAMPTON RACE CIRCUIT

Bridgehampton, Long Island, New York

THE COURSE: A fast 2.85-mile road circuit, asphalt-paved, ranging from 27' to 50' in width. Longest straight is 3100'. The public roads in and around Bridgehampton were the scene of many historic races in 1915–1921, and again from 1949 to 1953. The present closed course opened in 1957. It is an extremely challenging one—studded with hairpins, fast downhill sections, and high-speed bends.

SPECTATOR AREAS: Excellent spectator facilities. Choicest viewing areas are those inside the course along the long loop behind the pit area.

LAP RECORD: 1:39.6 (103 mph.), Lola Type 70

RESTRICTIONS: Law prohibits racing before 2 P.M. on Sunday.

FACILITIES: Parking for 6000 cars. Parking included in admission price, additional fees for grandstands and paddock. Refreshments and johns.

SANCTION: FIA, SCCA, LISCA.

ANNUAL EVENTS:

USRRC Race, May.

FIA-SCCA Race for GT cars, Sept. An international championship race dubbed "The Bridgehampton Double 500."

SCCA National and/or Regional Races.

TRAVEL DIRECTIONS: Bridgehampton is on the extreme eastern end of Long Island. From N. Y. C. (105 miles) take Midtown Tunnel to L. I. Expwy., Expwy. E. to Veteran's Memorial Hwy., Hwy. S. to Sunrise Hwy., Hwy. E. to Rte. 27 into Bridgehampton. Course is app. 3. miles N. of center of town, off Millstone Rd. Allow plenty of time when traveling on weekends. L. I. parkways are often clogged.

OWNER: Bridgehampton Enterprises, Inc., Bridgehampton, N. Y.

INFORMATION: About both events and accommodations, from Bridgehampton Enterprises, Inc., Bridgehampton, L. I., N. Y. Organization maintains a mailing list—ask to be put on it. Phone at circuit: 516—537-1414.

(Left) The straight that leads up to the Bridgehampton finish line. (Salt water behind explains the course's many sand dunes). (Below) Downhill sweep on the back stretch.

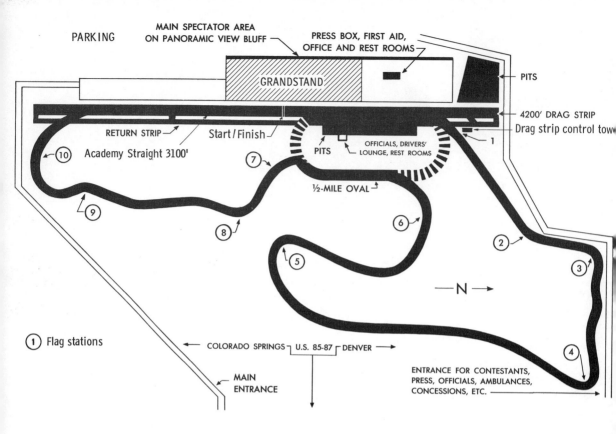

CONTINENTAL DIVIDE RACEWAYS

Castle Rock, Colorado

THE COURSE: One of the really fine racing circuits in the U.S., opened in
1959. 2.8 miles in length, asphalt-paved, varies between 30' and 85' in
width. Longest straight (in front of the main spectator area) is 3100'.
The raceways also include a ½-mile banked oval and a drag strip.

SPECTATOR AREAS: The view at Continental Divide is superb. Main spectator area, with concrete grandstand, is on a raised bluff opposite the
straight from which almost all of the circuit can be seen. Binoculars are
in order for best view of far turns. So are hats, for those sensitive to sun.
Additional spectator areas on the far side of the course offer closer view
of bends and turns, but do not command entire course.

LAP RECORD: 1:95 (app. 83 mph.), Lola-Chevrolet

RESTRICTIONS: None.

FACILITIES: Parking for 30,000 cars. Parking included in admission fee.
Additional fees sometimes charged for paddock admission. Refreshments
and johns.

SANCTION: SCCA, FIA, National Hot Rod Association, USAC

ANNUAL EVENTS:
 Colorado Grand Prix, May. SCCA Formula cars.
 Continental 250, June. USAC late model stock cars.
 USRRC Race, August.
 SCCA Regional and National Races.

OWNER: S. R. Langsam, Continental Divide Raceways, Security Life Bldg., Denver, Colo. Phone: 303—244-8037.

INFORMATION: Contact owner, above.

Spectator bluff at the Continental Divide commands almost the entire course.

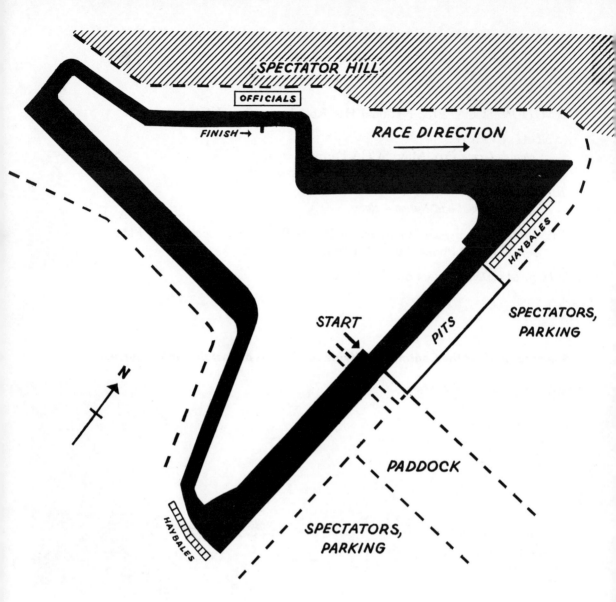

CUMBERLAND

Municipal Airport, Cumberland, Maryland

THE COURSE: This 1.6-mile airport course is macadam-paved, 50' wide, and includes a 2200' straight. The first sports car races were held there in May 1952 and have become an annual event, now of SCCA National Championship stature. The course includes seven turns, ranging from hairpin to relatively fast.

SPECTATOR AREAS: Cumberland is the exception to the "poor visibility at airport courses" rule. The whole of the course may be seen from a spectator hillside bordering the field. Binoculars recommended for viewing from the hill. Spectators not allowed inside course.

LAP RECORD: 1:11 (81.2 mph.), over 1600 cc. modified.

RESTRICTIONS: None.

FACILITIES: Parking for 10,000 cars. Parking fee included in admission. Camping permitted. Extra charge for paddock and camping.

SANCTION: SCCA.

ANNUAL EVENTS: SCCA National Race in May.

TRAVEL DIRECTIONS: The Municipal Airport is 2½ miles south of Cumberland, near Rte. 28. From Philadelphia (220 mi.) take Pa. Tpke. west to Exit 11 (U.S. 220), U.S. 220 south to Cumberland. From Pittsburgh (105 mi.) take Pa. Tpke. east to Exit 11. From Baltimore (135 mi.) take U.S. 40 west through Hagerstown. From Washington (135 mi.) take U.S. 50 west to W. Va. 28, north to Cumberland.

OWNER: City of Cumberland.

INFORMATION: For information about events, write SCCA, Steel Cities Region, c/o Mrs. F. Reynolds, Reynolds Sports Car Center, Rte. 30, Irwin, Pa. About accommodations, write Cumberland Lions Foundation, Box 1009, Cumberland, Md. PArkview 2-0123.

Straight at Cumberland, just past the esses that follow the finish line. Part of spectator hill can be seen at right.

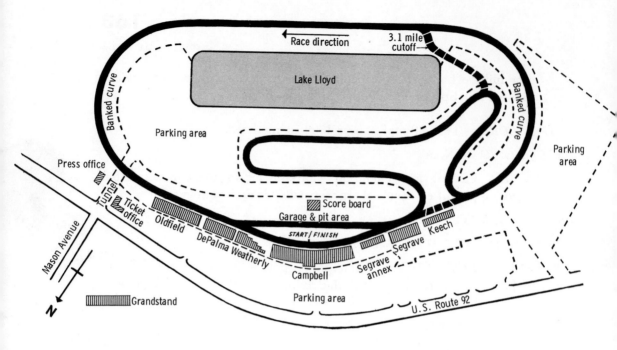

Race direction

3.1 mile cutoff →

Lake Lloyd

Banked curve

Banked curve

Parking area

Press office

Tunnel

Ticket office

Parking area

Score board

Garage & pit area

Oldfield

DePalma Weatherly

START/FINISH

Segrave

Keech

Campbell

Segrave annex

Mason Avenue

N

Grandstand

Parking area

U.S. Route 92

Daytona Beach, Florida

THE COURSE: The fast, 3.81 mile sports car course at Daytona Speedway opened in 1959; is made up of most of an outside, banked tri-oval track, plus a flat infield road section. It is asphalt paved, 40' to 60' wide, with a 3400' straight. Course may be shortened to 3.1 or 1.63 miles.

SPECTATOR AREAS: Daytona boasts 7 grandstands, each appropriately named after a famous driver, seating 50,000 in all. Campbell grandstand is opposite the start/finish line and offers a good view of the pit area as well. Far right-hand grandstand (Keech grandstand) is best for viewing the two sharp corners where the interior road course leaves and rejoins the tri-oval. Various infield areas are open to spectators.

LAP RECORD: 1:59.1 (115.2 mph.), Lotus-Ford, 3.81 mi. course.

Aerial view of Daytona shows vast orderly layout. This shot was taken during a stock car race on the tri-oval, so parked cars in infield have partially obscured interior road section.

RESTRICTIONS: None.

FACILITIES: Parking for 35,000 cars, extra charge for infield parking. Paddock tickets are available. Refreshments and johns. At major events infield tickets usually run $3 to $5; grandstands from $5 to $20. Seats in Campbell and Weatherly grandstands are most expensive, with the exception of ten top rows in Oldfield, De Palma, and Segrave stands.

SANCTION: FIA, SCCA, USAC, NASCAR, ARCA, USMC, AMA.

ANNUAL EVENTS:

Daytona Continental, February. 24 hour. FIA race for sports, prototype, and GT cars. Counts toward International Manufacturer's Championship.

SSCA National Races. Frequent *stock and speedway car races* on tri-oval . . . at 170 mph. and up!

TRAVEL DIRECTIONS: Daytona Speedway is located 2 mi. W. of Daytona Beach on U.S. 92. From Jacksonville (90 mi.) take U.S. 1 south. From Miami (260 mi.) take Sunshine State Pkwy. north to U.S. 1. From Orlando (60 mi.) take Interstate 4 to U.S. 92 to Speedway.

OWNER: Daytona International Speedway Corp., William H. G. France, Pres., Drawer S, Daytona Beach.

INFORMATION: Write Houston Lawing, Public Relations Director of the Corp., above, for information about events, or to have your name put on their mailing list. Chamber of Commerce, Daytona Beach (CLinton 2-4723), will help with accommodations.

nfield section of Daytona looks just like any other road course. The banked ection is the unusual part.

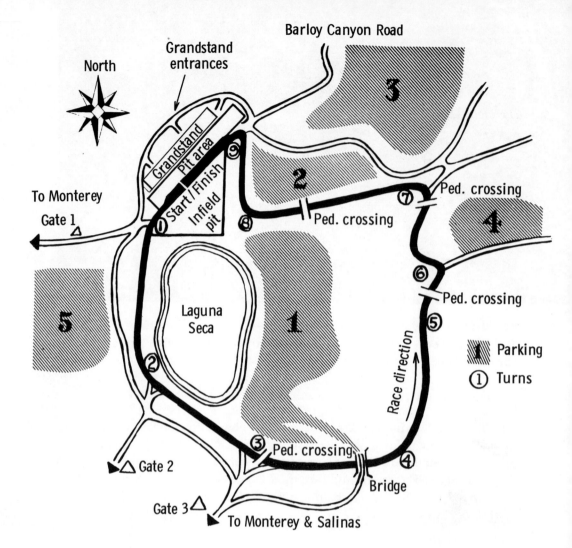

LAGUNA SECA

Monterey, California

THE COURSE: A tricky 1.9 mile road course, asphalt-paved, an average 30′ wide with a 1200′ straight. Course opened in 1957. It has 9 turns, including two banked S-turns and one 130 degree hairpin (Turn #9).

SPECTATOR AREAS: Excellent visibility from hills both inside and outside the circuit. From two vantage points, more than 85 per cent of the course can be seen. Binoculars recommended for more distant sections. All turns exciting, but Numbers 2, 6, 7, and 9 are particularly so.

LAP RECORD:
  1:12.8 (96 mph.) under 2000 cc. (Elva-Porsche)
  1:07.0 (102.1 mph.) over 2000 cc. (Chaparral)

USRRC Race at Laguna Seca really packs in the crowds.

RESTRICTIONS: None

FACILITIES: Parking for 20,000 cars. Parking included in admission price. Extra charge for paddock passes. Refreshments and johns.

SANCTION: SCCA, FIA.

ANNUAL EVENTS:
   USRRC Race, May.
   Monterey Grand Prix, International SCCA/FIA event, October.

TRAVEL DIRECTIONS: Course is located on Fort Ord Reservation between Monterey and Salinas. From San Francisco (120 mi.), take U.S. 101 south. From Los Angeles (320 mi.), take U.S. 101 north.

PROMOTER: Sports Car Racing Assoc. of Monterey Peninsula (SCRAMP), a non-profit corporation which donates proceeds to area charities.

INFORMATION: From SCRAMP, P.O. Box 781, Monterey, Calif. 93942. Phone: 408—373-1811. Gen'l. Mgr. is Ned Simpson. About accommodations, write Visitors Bureau, P.O. Box 489, Monterey. Phone: 408—375-2252.

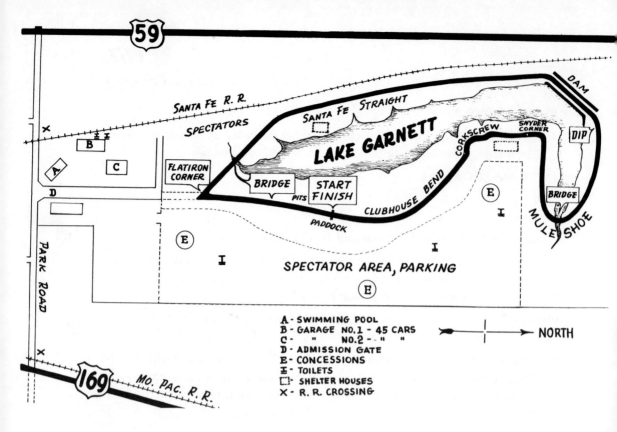

LAKE GARNETT

Garnett, Kansas

THE COURSE: A relatively level, 2.84-mile road course that runs through Garnett City Park around the shores of Lake Garnett. The surface is asphalt, an average 27′ wide. Course opened in 1959. Longest straight is the back or "Santa Fe" straight: 1 mile.

SPECTATOR AREAS: Best areas are those near Mule Shoe, the Clubhouse Bend, and Flatiron Corner.

LAP RECORD: App. 1:47 (app. 95 mph.).

RESTRICTIONS: No spectator towers or scaffolds permitted.

FACILITIES: Parking for 30,000 cars, parking fee included in admission price. Extra charge for paddock passes. Refreshments and johns. Many pleasant picnicking spots, plus a swimming pool, in the Park.

SANCTION: SCCA.

ANNUAL EVENTS: Lake Garnett Grand Prix, July. (The Grand Prix is a National Championship SCCA event.) No race held in 1965.

TRAVEL DIRECTIONS: Garnett is in eastern Kansas, approx. 35 mi. from the Missouri border. From Kansas City, Kansas (75 mi.), take U.S. 169. From Wichita (145 mi.) take U.S. 54 to U.S. 59, U.S. 59 to Garnett. Course is just north of intersection of U.S. 59 and U.S. 169.

OWNER: City of Garnett.

INFORMATION: Write Frank H. Bennett, Publ. Dir., Lake Garnett Grand Prix Sports Car Racing Association, Garnett, Kansas for information about events. Association maintains a mailing list for news of coming events. For information about accommodations, write Garnett Chamber of Commerce, Garnett, Kansas.

(Above) Jam-packed paddock at Lake Garnett. (Below) Modified machinery battles it out in the tight, tricky Corkscrew.

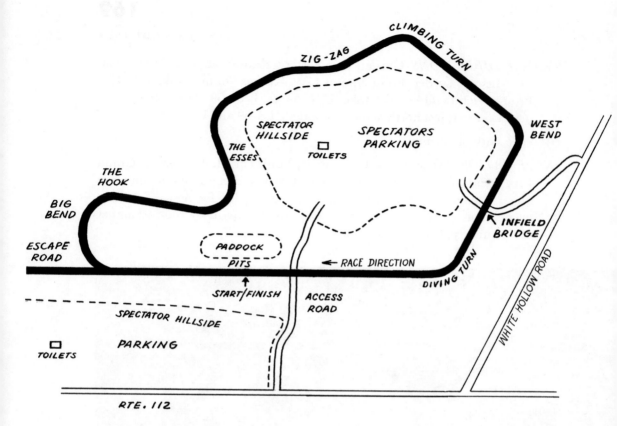

LIME ROCK PARK

Lime Rock, Connecticut

THE COURSE: A closed road circuit, 1.5 miles long, with a 2750′ straight. The course, one of the country's most beautiful, was opened in 1957. Surface is asphalt, 30′ wide. Circuit includes several sharp corners, fast bends, esses, a climbing uphill turn, and a fast downhill swing that ends in the straight.

SPECTATOR AREAS: Lime Rock's are unsurpassed. The course encloses a hill whose partially shaded banks make perfect natural grandstands. Preferred location is the grassy hillside that overlooks the esses. Almost all of the course can be seen by moving about in the relatively small infield. The hillside opposite the pit area offers an excellent view of the start/finish and the straight, as well as of the hard right-hand corner at the end of the straight.

LAP RECORD: 1:01.8 (app. 87 mph.), Cooper-Alfa.

Small production cars stir up a cloud going through Lime Rock's esses. Infield spectator hillside in the background.

RESTRICTIONS: Law prohibits racing at night or on Sundays.

FACILITIES: Parking for 10,000 cars, with parking included in admission price. Additional fee for paddock passes. No grandstands. Refreshments and johns.

SANCTION: SCCA, LISCA (Long Island Sports Car Assoc.), BSCOA (British Sports Car Owners Assoc.)

ANNUAL EVENTS:
   SCCA National and Regional Races.
   LISCA and BSCOA Races.
   SCCA, LISCA and BSCOA Driver's Schools.

TRAVEL DIRECTIONS: Lime Rock is in the northwest corner of Conn., on Conn. 112 off U.S. 7. From New York (100 mi.) take Taconic State Pkwy. to U.S. 44, U.S. 44 to Conn. 343, Conn. 343 to Conn. 41, Conn. 41 to Conn. 112. From Boston (150 mi.) take Mass. Tpke. to Lee (Exit 2), Mass. 102 to Stockbridge, U.S. 7 to Conn. 112.

OWNER: Lime Rock Corp., Lime Rock, Conn., James Haynes, Pres. Phone: 203—HE5-2572.

INFORMATION: Write Lime Rock Park, Lime Rock, Conn., for information about events. Phone, same as above. To get on the course's mailing list, fill out blank included in the program at each event.

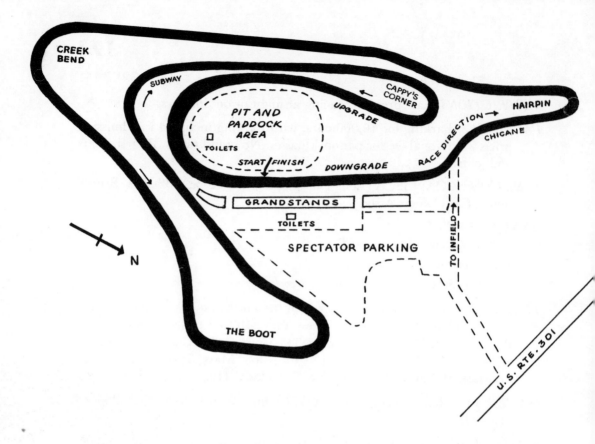

MARLBORO MOTOR RACEWAY

Upper Marlboro, Maryland

THE COURSE: 1.8 miles of tightly twisting black-top, 25–45' wide. The course is relatively level, with its longest straight running some 2500'. Race direction is counter-clockwise, unlike most American sports car circuits. The course opened in 1955.

SPECTATOR AREAS: Limited primarily to the vicinity of the grandstands. Grandstands themselves are recommended, as their height commands an excellent (and otherwise unobtainable) view of a considerable part of the course.

LAP RECORD: 1:30 (app. 68 mph.), Lotus-Alfa.

RESTRICTIONS: None.

FACILITIES: Parking for 2000 cars. Admission price includes parking. Only entrants are allowed in pit/paddock area. Refreshments and johns.

SANCTION: SCCA, FIA.

Porsches and Alfas slither along Marlboro's rain-swept macadam. Proximity of various stretches of the course is typical of Marlboro.

ANNUAL EVENTS:

Marlboro Twelve Hour, SCCA/FIA sedan race.

SCCA National Races, April, July, September.

SCCA Regional Races, almost year round.

SCCA Drivers Schools.

TRAVEL DIRECTIONS: Course is located in Upper Marlboro on U.S. 301. From Washington, D. C. (15 mi.), take Suitland Parkway east to Rte. 4, Rte. 4 to U.S. 301. From Baltimore (40 mi.) take U.S. 301 south. From Richmond (105 mi.) take U.S. 301 north.

OWNER: Marlboro Park Speedway, Les Netherton, Pres. P.O. Box 33, Upper Marlboro, Md. 20870. Phone: 301—627-3333.

INFORMATION: About events, write owner, above, or SCCA Washington, D. C. Region, 734 Fifteenth St., N.W., Washington, D. C. Phone: RE 7-1990. Ample accommodations in the area.

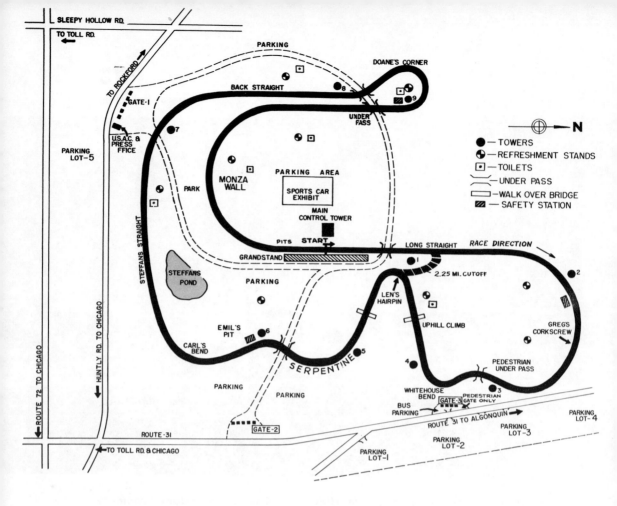

MEADOWDALE INTERNATIONAL RACEWAYS

Carpentersville, Illinois

THE COURSE: A 3.27-mile road course opened in 1958. It's asphalt-paved, 32′ wide, and includes both uphill and downhill sections, hairpins, esses, a 4000′ straight, and a banked 180 degree turn: the "Monza Wall." Course may also be shortened to 2.25 miles.

SPECTATOR AREAS: Many and excellent. One of the best is inside the far right-hand loop, from which both the end of the straight and the downhill right-hand turn may be seen. The "Monza Wall" is in full view from both the grandstand and the parking/spectator area it partially encloses.

LAP RECORD: App. 1:59 (app. 98.7 mph.), 3.27 mi. course, over 1600 cc.

RESTRICTIONS: None.

FACILITIES: Parking for 30,000 cars. No extra charge for parking or grand-stand seats, but paddock passes are additional. Refreshments and johns.

SANCTION: SCCA and others.

ANNUAL EVENTS:
    SCCA National Races.
    SCCA Regional Races.
    Occasional *club* and *stock car* races.

TRAVEL DIRECTIONS: Carpentersville is 45 mi. northwest of Chicago on Ill. 31, 3 mi. north of Elgin. From Chicago, take Northwest Tollway to Ill. 31.

LESSEE: Mid-America Auto Racing, Inc., Ralph Banghart, Pres., 63 West Schiller St., Chicago 10, Ill. Phone: 312—MI2-8576.

INFORMATION: From lessee, above, about both events and accommodations. Mailing list maintained.

(Above) Meadowdale's "Monza Wall," named after the famous Italian course near Milan. (Right) The end of the 4000' straight.

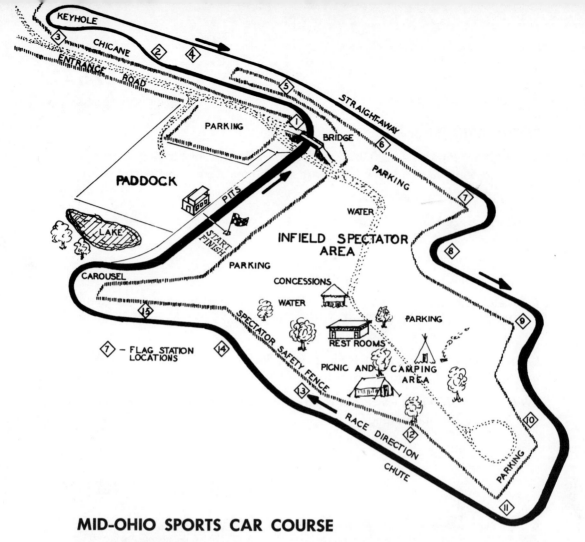

MID-OHIO SPORTS CAR COURSE

Lexington, Ohio

THE COURSE: A tight, 2.4 mile asphalt-paved course set in the lovely rolling country of central Ohio. The longest straight is a bit over three-quarters of a mile. A relative newcomer among U.S. circuits, the course opened in 1962, and saw its first major event, a USRRC race, in 1963.

SPECTATOR AREAS: No grandstands, but much of the interior of the course is open to spectators.

LAP RECORDS:
    1:44.2 (82.92 mph.), under 2000 cc. mod. (Elva-BMW)
    1:40.6 (85.88 mph.), over 2000 cc. mod. (Chaparral)

RESTRICTIONS: None.

FACILITIES: Parking for approx. 10,000 cars. Admission price includes parking. Extra charge for pits and paddock. Refreshments and johns.

SANCTION: SCCA, FIA

ANNUAL EVENTS:

    USRRC Race, August.

    SCCA National Races, June and July.

    SCCA Regional Races and *Drivers Schools.*

    Occasional *stock car* and *go-kart* events.

TRAVEL DIRECTIONS: Mid-Ohio is located on Steam Corners Road in Lexington, Ohio, approx. 8 mi. SW of Mansfield. From Cleveland (70 mi.), take Interstate 71 south. From Akron (60 mi.), Interstate 80 SW. to Interstate 71, then south. From Columbus (50 mi.), take Interstate 71 north.

OWNER: Mid-Ohio Sports, Inc., Les Griebling, Pres., 36 West Main St., Lexington, Ohio 44904. Phone: 419—884-2295.

INFORMATION: About both events and accommodations, from owner, above. Course maintains a mailing list.

A smoking start from the Mid-Ohio grid.

Mid-Ohio's surroundings are lush and green.

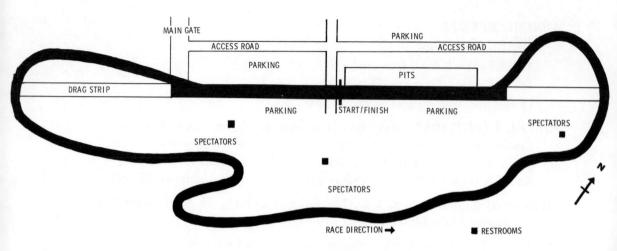

PACIFIC RACEWAYS

Kent, Washington

THE COURSE: 2.25 miles of winding asphalt, with one straight of approximately .4 mile. Pavement varies between 40′ and 90′ in width, with an elevation change of almost 200′. Pacific Raceways opened in 1960. It is an extremely challenging course, since almost three-fourths of its length is composed of turns, bends, and hairpins. A go-kart course and .5 mi. drag-racing strip are also within the 200 acre area.

SPECTATOR AREAS: A 5000-seat grandstand and the shady hillsides within the course provide superb spectator vantage points.

LAP RECORD: 1:20 (app. 99 mph.) McLaren-Olds.

FACILITIES: Parking for 10,000 cars. No extra charge for parking. Spectators admitted to paddock for additional charge. Refreshments and johns.

RESTRICTIONS: None.

SANCTION: FIA, SCCA, USAC.

ANNUAL EVENTS:

    Grand Prix for Sports Cars, Intern'l. SCCA/FIA event, October.

    USRRC Race, July.

    SCCA National and Regional Races.

TRAVEL DIRECTIONS: Pacific Raceways is located 5 miles east of the center of Kent. From Seattle (25 mi.) take U.S. 99 south to Rte. 5A, then east on 5A. From Tacoma (25 mi.) take U.S. 99 north to Rte. 5A, then east on 5A.

OWNER: Pacific Raceways, Inc., P.O. Box 146, Kent, Wash. UL 2-2133.

INFORMATION: About events, from owner, above. Course maintains a mailing list.

Esses and bends make a real "drivers' course" out of the back section of Pacific Raceways.

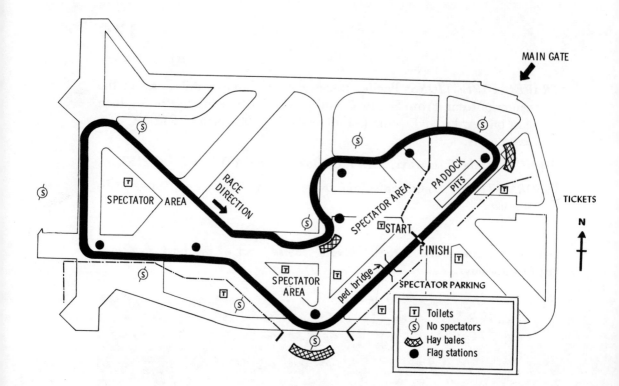

PENSACOLA FIESTA OF FIVE FLAGS
SPORTS CAR RACING COURSE

Pensacola, Florida

THE COURSE: A demanding 3-mile airport course laid out on Pensacola's
  Corry Field. The course is concrete, with a minimum width of 50′ and
  two straights. One is the 4500′ stretch that passes the pits, the other a
  one-quarter-mile back straight.

SPECTATOR AREAS: Best areas are in the neighborhoods of the start/finish
  line and the back "S" turns. Paddock area is open to spectators, as is the
  interior of most of the circuit.

LAP RECORD: 1:45.2 (108 mph.), Lola Type 70.

RESTRICTIONS: None.

FACILITIES: Parking for 30,000 cars. Admission price includes parking.
  Extra charge for paddock passes. Refreshments and johns.

SANCTION: SCCA.

ANNUAL EVENTS: USRRC Race, April.

TRAVEL DIRECTIONS: Corry Field is in Warrington, Fla., a few miles south of intersection of U.S. 90 and 98 at West Pensacola. From New Orleans (200 mi.) or Mobile (60 mi.) drive via U.S. 90.

OWNER: U.S. Navy, Naval Air Station, Pensacola.

INFORMATION: Write Fiesta of Five Flags Assoc., 370 Brent Bldg., Pensacola, Fla., for information about events and accommodations. Association maintains a mailing list. Phone: 305—HE3-6512.

Pensacola is typical of many airport courses: is marked by wide-open concrete spaces, plenty of room to maneuver.

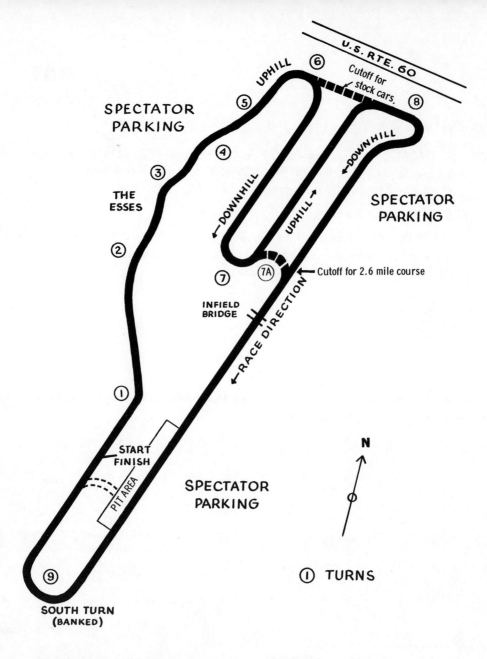

RIVERSIDE INTERNATIONAL RACEWAY

Edgemont, California

THE COURSE: A 3.275 mile closed-road course, asphalt-paved, 60' wide with 14' shoulders. Shortened to a 2.6 mile course for major sports car events. For stock car racing, an alternate course is used in which cars go directly from Turn 6 to Turn 8. All variations include a banked turn 60' wide (South Turn).

SPECTATOR AREAS: Many and varied. Spectators permitted around the major part of the course.

LAP RECORD: 1:26.6 (app. 108 mph.), McLaren-Olds, 2.6 mi. course.

RESTRICTIONS: None.

FACILITIES: Paved parking for 65,000 cars, total parking area for 100,000 cars. Refreshments and johns. Reserved grandstands $2.00 and $2.50.

SANCTION: SCCA, FIA, Amer. Motorcycle Assoc., NASCAR, Nat'l. Hot Rod Assoc.

ANNUAL EVENTS:
  USRRC Race, May.
  Los Angeles Times Grand Prix, International SCCA/FIA event.
  Riverside 500, January, an intern'l. NASCAR/FIA stock car event.

TRAVEL DIRECTIONS: Riverside is located 5 miles east of Riverside, California, east of the intersection of U.S. 60 and 395, ½ mile north of March Field. From Los Angeles (60 mi.), take San Bernadino Freeway east. From San Diego (95 mi.), take U.S. 395 north.

OWNER: Riverside International Raceway, Inc.

INFORMATION: From owner, above, 6067 Hollywood Blvd., Los Angeles, Calif. Phone: 213—466-1684. Or 22255 Eucalyptus Ave., Riverside. Phone: 714—653-1161 or 714—684-4200. For information about accommodations, write Riverside Chamber of Commerce, 4261 Main St., Riverside.

Potent machinery and top drivers draw big Riverside crowds.

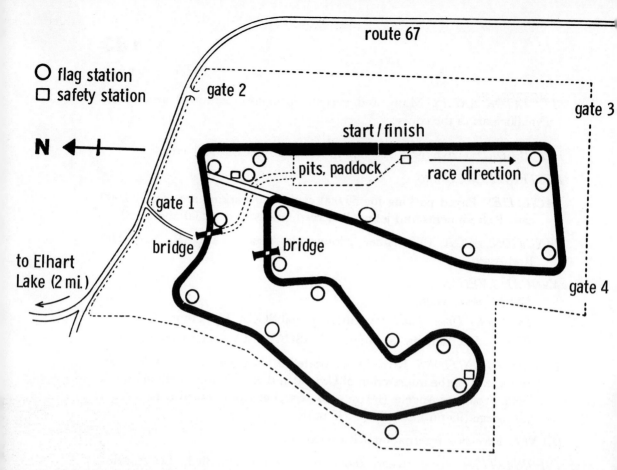

ROAD AMERICA

Elkhart Lake, Wisconsin

THE COURSE: Exactly 4 miles of twisting, 27′-wide blacktop, with a 4300′ straight. The present course opened in 1955, after several years of racing on county roads in the area. One of the most famous of American courses, Road America has earned much of its fame through its annual 500-mile sports car race.

SPECTATOR AREAS: Over 7 miles of viewing area, much of it on grassy countryside. Road America is an excellent course to roam, as the circuit's variety is almost infinite. Grandstand not recommended, unless you *must* see the start and finish.

LAP RECORD: 2:28 (app. 97 mph.), Chaparral

RESTRICTIONS: None.

FACILITIES: Parking area of 150 acres. Parking and grandstand fees included in admission price. Extra charge for paddock passes. Many people bring their own picnic lunches. Refreshments and johns.

Few courses offer such a blend of pleasant countryside and difficult racing as Road America.

SANCTION: SCCA, FIA.

ANNUAL EVENTS:
> *Road America June Sprints,* SCCA National races.
> *Road America "500",* September—a USRRC race.

TRAVEL DIRECTIONS: Road America is on Wisc. 67, 2 mi. south of Elkhart Lake. From Milwaukee (55 mi.), take U.S. 141 north to Wisc. 57, Wisc. 57 to Wisc. 23 (near Plymouth), Wisc. 23 west to Wisc. 67.

OWNER: Elkhart Lake's Road America, Inc., Clif Tufte, Pres., Elkhart Lake, Wisconsin. TRinity 6-2900.

INFORMATION: From owner, above, about events. Mailing list maintained. Write Chamber of Commerce, Elkhart Lake, for information about accommodations.

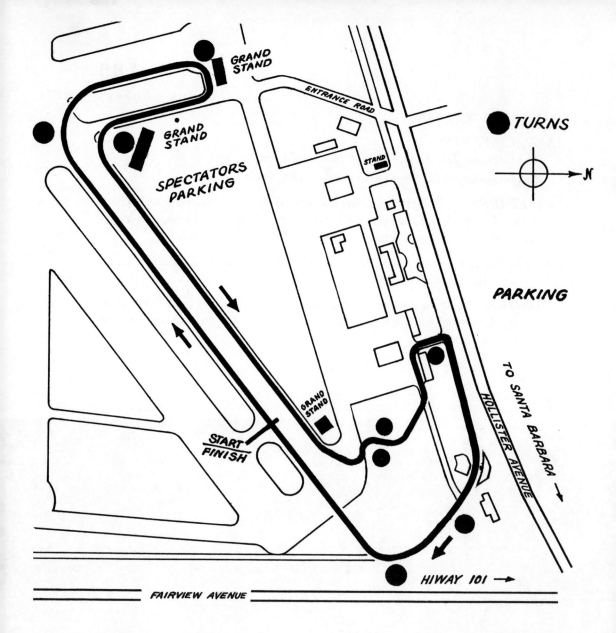

SANTA BARBARA

Santa Barbara, California

THE COURSE: A 2.5-mile course laid out over the landing strips and access roads of Goleta Airport. Paving is concrete and asphalt. Road width varies from 30′ to 150′. Longest straight is slightly over half a mile long. Races have been held at the airport since 1953.

Small modified cars have plenty of chance t mix it up in the loop at the western end of th Santa Barbara course.

SPECTATOR AREAS: As at all flat airport courses, it is difficult to see any large part of the course from any one point at Santa Barbara. However, several grandstands take the place of natural rises of land. Those at the turns at the end of the pit straight give an excellent view of much exciting cornering.

LAP RECORD: Record race average on previous 1.5 mile course: app. 1:08 (app. 80 mph.), over 1600 cc.

RESTRICTIONS: None.

FACILITIES: Parking for 15,000 cars. Parking fee included in admission price. Extra charge for grandstand seats. Refreshments and johns.

SANCTION: SCCA.

ANNUAL EVENTS:
SCCA Regional Races, May and September

TRAVEL DIRECTIONS: Course is in Goleta, 7 miles northwest of Santa Barbara. From San Francisco (340 mi.), take U.S. 101 south. From Los Angeles (100 mi.), Rte. 101 north.

OWNER: County of Santa Barbara, Santa Barbara, Calif.

INFORMATION: Write SCCA Cal Club Region, 3491 Cahuenga Blvd., Hollywood 28, Calif. Phone: 213—HO5-2002. Club maintains mailing list.

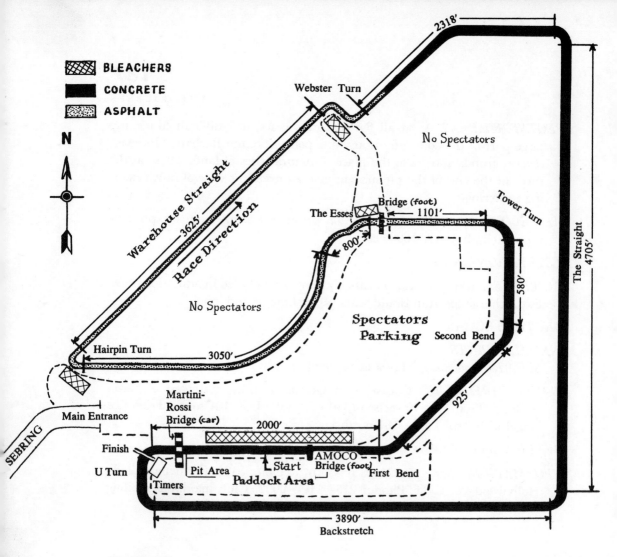

SEBRING

Sebring, Florida

THE COURSE: A 5.2-mile course laid out on the runways and service roads of Sebring Air Terminal. Approximately one third of the course is asphalt-paved, the remainder is concrete. Course includes three long straights: 3600′, 3900′, and 4700′. All three straights end in slow, right-angle turns, a layout that makes the course extremely hard on brakes. Present course was first used in 1952.

SPECTATOR AREAS: The entire interior loop bounded by the Martini-Rossi Bridge, First and Second Bends, Tower Bend, the Esses and the Hairpin Turn is open to spectators. There are also small spectator areas near the Esses and the Webster Turn. Since the course is flat, a bleacher seat increases the view. Many pit stops make the bleachers opposite the pit area very desirable.

Sebring's pit straight at dusk, from th
Martini-Rossi bridge. Annual Twelve Hou
Grand Prix starts at 10 A.M., so severa
hours of night racing are always included

LAP RECORD: 2:59.3 (104.4 mph.), Chaparral.

RESTRICTIONS: None.

FACILITIES: Unlimited parking. For 12-Hour Grand Prix, parking is included in general admission ($4 per person). Bleacher seats $3–4 extra. Paddock pass $8 extra. Preferred parking areas along course $12 and up, plus general admission. Box seat above pits (including paddock pass and general admission) is $24. Refreshments and johns.

ANNUAL EVENTS:
12-Hour Florida International Grand Prix of Endurance (FIA-SCCA), March. By all odds, one of the most important U.S. sports car races. Counts toward the International Manufacturers' Championship.

TRAVEL DIRECTIONS: The Sebring Air Terminal is located 5 miles east of Sebring near U.S. 98 in central Florida. From Miami (160 mi.) take U.S. 27 northwest. From Orlando (100 mi.) take U.S. 17 south to Davenport, Rte. 547 west 1 mi. to U.S. 27, U.S. 27 south to Sebring. Note: Seaboard Air Line trains to Miami go through Sebring and stop there.

OWNER: Sebring Air Terminal.

INFORMATION: About events: from Automobile Racing Club of Florida, Inc., P.O. Box 719, Sebring, Florida. About accommodations: from Accommodations Committee, Sebring, Florida. Reserve accommodations well in advance—Sebring and surrounding country are jammed during the annual event.

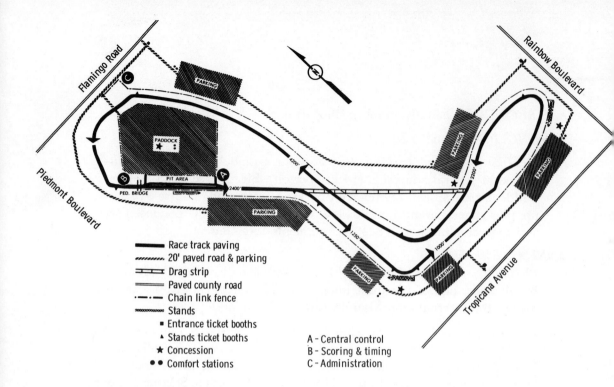

Legend:

- Race track paving
- 20' paved road & parking
- Drag strip
- Paved county road
- Chain link fence
- Stands
- ■ Entrance ticket booths
- ▲ Stands ticket booths
- ★ Concession
- ●● Comfort stations

A - Central control
B - Scoring & timing
C - Administration

STARDUST INTERNATIONAL RACEWAY

Las Vegas, Nevada

THE COURSE: Squarely in the middle of the Nevada desert lies one of the newest and finest of American circuits. Exactly 3 miles long, it's dead level, an average 35' wide, and asphalt-paved. The longest straight is 4200'. Opened in 1965, its first major race proved it to be the second fastest U.S. road course—second only to Daytona.

SPECTATOR AREAS: Because Stardust is level, the best views are from the grandstands. One grandstand gives an excellent view of cars leaving the Esses as well as their slides through the hairpin.

LAP RECORD: 1:38 (110.2 mph.), Chaparral.

RESTRICTIONS: None.

FACILITIES: Parking for 15,000 cars; no additional charge for parking. General admission is $3–5 at major events. Additional charge of $2–4 for grandstands. Paddock passes available at extra cost. Refreshments and johns.

SANCTION: FIA, SCCA.

Well-paved, well-organized paddock at Stardust.

ANNUAL EVENTS:
  USRRC Race, spring.
  Stardust Grand Prix, FIA/SCCA, late fall.
  SCCA Regional races, spring and fall

TRAVEL DIRECTIONS: Stardust is located 6 mi. W. of the "Strip" in Las Vegas. From downtown Las Vegas, take U.S. 91 S. to Spring Mt. Rd., then W. on Spring Mt. Rd. to Rainbow Blvd. Go S. on Rainbow Blvd. ¾ mi. to Flamingo Rd., then W. on Flamingo Rd. to main gate.

OWNER: Stardust Racing Assoc., Leo Margolian, Gen'l Mgr., Stardust Hotel, Las Vegas, Nevada. Phone: 702—735-6269.

INFORMATION: Write owner, above. Course maintains a mailing list—ask to be put on it.

Stardust, like Sebring, has a Martini & Rossi bridge. But mountain backdrop is strictly from Nevada.

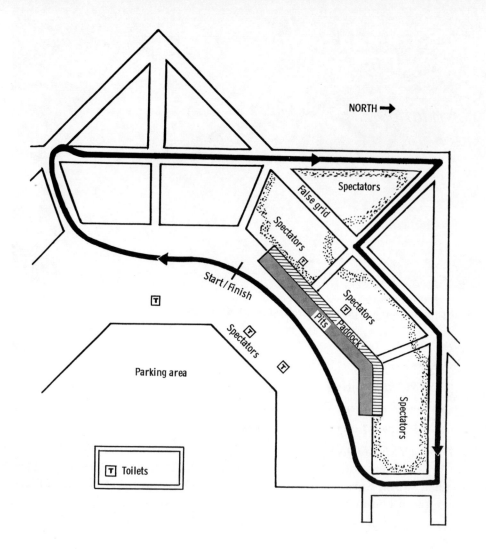

STUTTGART

Air Base, Stuttgart, Arkansas

THE COURSE: A fast airport course, 2.6 miles in length. Surface is concrete, with a minimum width of 50'. Longest straight is 3900', but the course also includes 5000' of gentle high-speed curve. Course opened in 1959, with a somewhat different layout.

SPECTATOR AREAS: No grandstands, but a considerable portion of the grassy infield is open to spectators. Area opposite the starting line is most popular with spectators.

LAP RECORD: App. 1:41 (app. 93 mph.), Lotus Thirty.

RESTRICTIONS: None.

FACILITIES: Parking for 10,000 cars. Admission price includes parking. Only additional cost (optional) is for admission to the paddock: one dollar per person (no cars). Refreshments and johns.

SANCTION: SCCA.

ANNUAL EVENTS: Grand Prairie Grand Prix, April. An SCCA National race.

TRAVEL DIRECTIONS: Stuttgart Air Base is located 6 mi. north of Stuttgart on Arkansas Rte. 11. From Little Rock (55 mi.) take U.S. 70 east to Arkansas Rte. 11, then south on Rte. 11 to Airport. From Memphis, Tenn. (110 mi.) take U.S. 70 or U.S. 79 southwest to Rte. 11.

OWNER: City of Stuttgart.

INFORMATION: About events: from Dr. Jim Bisbee, Box 389, Stuttgart, Arkansas. Phone: WA 3-4461. For accommodations, write Stuttgart Junior Chamber of Commerce, Box 53, Stuttgart.

East end of the circuit at Stuttgart, with cars ready on the grid.

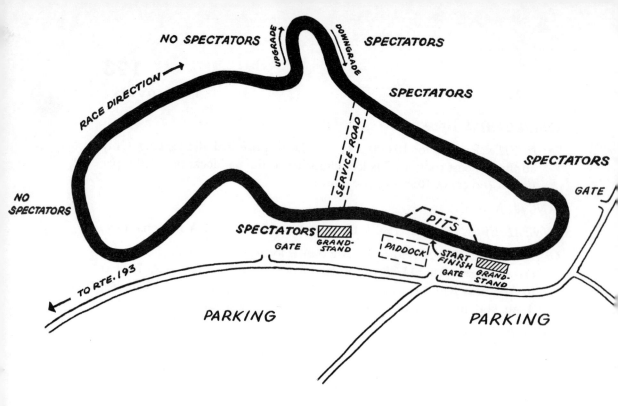

THOMPSON RACEWAY

Thompson, Connecticut

THE COURSE: Two twisting miles of asphalt-paved road course, 27' wide, with dirt shoulders. Escape areas on all corners. Present course opened in 1952. Longest straight is 0.6 mile long.

SPECTATOR AREAS: Best spots are those marked "Spectators" on the map. The one at upper center gives an excellent view of a fast downhill bend, the one at far right overlooks a very slow hairpin, and the one at lower center is opposite both the downhill section of the straight and the linked left and right turns at its end.

LAP RECORD: 1:36 (app. 76 mph.), Cooper-Ford.

RESTRICTIONS: Law prohibits racing at night.

FACILITIES: Parking for 3000 cars. Admission price includes parking, but not grandstands, for which an extra fee is charged. Refreshments and johns. No spectators admitted to paddock.

SANCTION: SCCA and others.

ANNUAL EVENTS:
    SCCA National Races, Labor Day Weekend.
    SCCA Regional Races, spring, summer, fall.
    SCCA Drivers Schools.

Slow corner at the end of the back straight is popular with spectators.

TRAVEL DIRECTIONS: Thompson Raceway is in the northeast corner of Connecticut, 2 mi. north of Thompson, off Conn. 193. From New York City (175 mi.) take Conn. Tpke. to Danielson, Conn. (almost at the end of Tpke.), Conn. 12 north to Conn. 21, Conn. 21 to Conn. 193. Stay on 193 through Thompson to Raceway. From Boston (60 mi.), take Mass. 16 to Rte. 193 (1 mi. east of Webster, Mass.), south on Rte. 193 to Thompson. Or Mass. Tpke. to Auburn Exit, then Rte. 12 south.

OWNER: Thompson Raceway, Inc., Box 99, Thompson, Conn. George B. Weaver, Sec.-Treas.-Mgr., WAlnut 3-9219.

INFORMATION: From owner, above, about events. They also send out excellent, informative postcards with news of coming events to those who request them. Accommodations available at Vernon Stiles Inn, Thompson, and at many cabins, hotels, and motels in the area. Chamber of Commerce, Putnam, Conn., can help with suggestions.

The demanding uphill-downhill hairpin at Thompson.

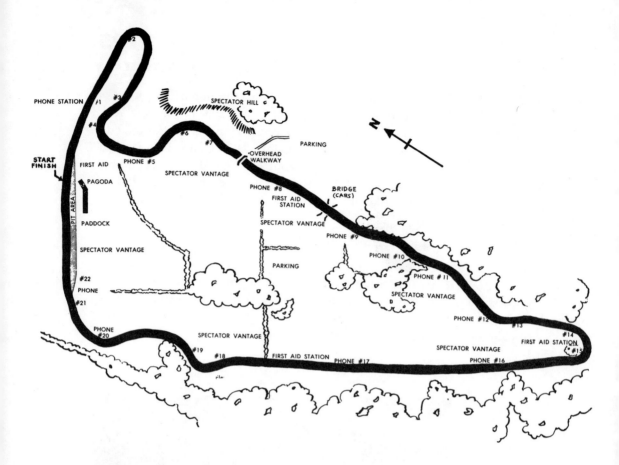

VIRGINIA INTERNATIONAL RACEWAY

Danville, Virginia

THE COURSE: 3.2 challenging miles of asphalt-paved road course through gently rolling countryside. Pavement is 27′ wide. Longest straight is 5000′. A wide variety of turns—twelve in all—is included in the course, which opened in 1957.

SPECTATOR AREAS: Much of the interior of the course is open to spectators, as well as the spectator hill outside the course (upper left on the map). One of the most popular areas inside the course is that opposite the left- and right-hand bends at the end of the straight on the west side of the course.

LAP RECORD: App. 2:13 (app. 87 mph.) in a Maserati.

RESTRICTIONS: None.

FACILITIES: Unlimited parking. Parking included in admission price. Extra charge for paddock passes. Refreshments and johns.

Rolling country, plenty of demanding turns mark the V.I.R. circuit.

SANCTION: SCCA.

ANNUAL EVENTS:
    SCCA National Races, spring.
    SCCA Regional Races.

TRAVEL DIRECTIONS: Course is near Milton, N. C., 12 mi. southeast of Danville off N. C. 62. From Richmond (175 mi.) take U.S. 301 south to intersection with U.S. 58 (1 mi. north of Emporia, Va.), then U.S. 58 west to N. C. 62.

OWNER: VIR is operated by E. Paul Rembold and sponsored by the Danville Civil Air Patrol.

INFORMATION: For information about events at the course, write Virginia International Raceway, P.O. Box 47, Danville, Va., or to the sanctioning organization. The Danville Chamber of Commerce can supply information about accommodations in the area.

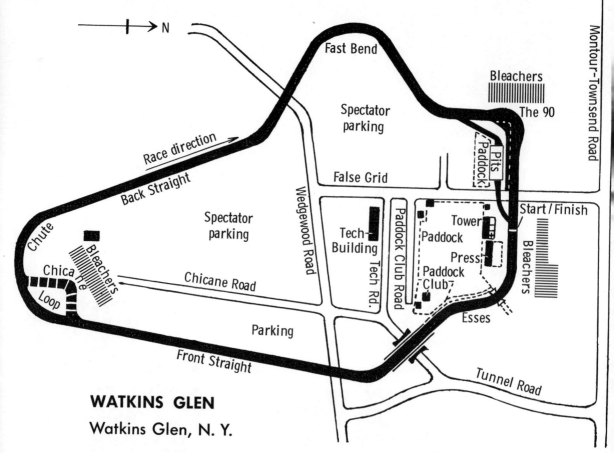

N

WATKINS GLEN

Watkins Glen, N. Y.

THE COURSE: A closed, 2.3-mile road course, asphalt-paved. Roadway is 26′ wide with 8′ oiled shoulders, and includes a gently curved back "straight" app. 0.7 miles long. Course has a chicane at its extreme south end, which is by-passed at some events. Present course (third of three in the area since 1948) opened in 1956.

SPECTATOR AREAS: Almost all of the course interior is open to spectators. Preferred areas are those in the neighborhood of the chicane, at the fast bend at the end of the back "straight," and near the sharp right-hand turn before the start/finish line.

LAP RECORD:
Sports Cars: 1:19.9 (103.6 mph.), Chaparral.
Formula One: 1:11.9 (115.2 mph.), BRM.
Note: Sports car record set on course with chicane included, Formula One record set on course with chicane bypassed.

RESTRICTIONS: Law prohibits racing on Sunday before 1:05 P.M.

FACILITIES: Almost unlimited parking, both within and without the circuit. Parking included in admission price, additional fees for bleachers. Refreshments and johns. Many spectators camp out at the course during two-day

Right-angle downhill turn near the pits at the Glen is tricky, as No. 143 has discovered.

Long, fast uphill sweep towards the Front Straight.

events. Course maintains a Paddock Club. Membership admits member to an enclosed, choice hillside viewing area with tent, bar service, and free food. Membership ($25 per person, $40 per couple, plus general admission fees) is valid at both Grand Prix and sports car events.

SANCTION: FIA, SCCA, NASCAR.

ANNUAL EVENTS:

Grand Prix of the United States, October (Formula I, FIA). The most important road-racing event in the United States—the only one held here which counts toward the International Driver's Championship.

Glen Grand Prix, June. A USRRC race.

SCCA National Races, August.

SCCA Regional Races.

TRAVEL DIRECTIONS: Watkins Glen is in west central New York State, on N.Y. 14. From New York City (275 mi.), N.Y. State Thruway to Harriman (Exit 16), N.Y. 17 or alternates to Horseheads, N.Y. (6 mi. N. of Elmira), N.Y. 14 to Watkins Glen.

OWNER: Watkins Glen Grand Prix Corporation, Watkins Glen, N.Y. Phone: 607—535-2000 or 607—535-2500.

INFORMATION: About events, from owners, who also maintain a mailing list. About accommodations: from Watkins Glen Chamber of Commerce, Watkins Glen, N.Y. Phone: 607—535-6546.

GOOD READING
ABOUT RACING

Magazines

ROAD AND TRACK   An authoritative monthly magazine crammed with road tests of new cars, technical features; reports on all major European Grand Prix and sports car races as well as most major U.S. races five to eight weeks after the race. Compiles many of its most important road tests in a handy Road Test Annual ($1). 60¢ on newsstands, one-year subscription $5 from R & T, 834 Production Place, Newport Beach, California.

CAR AND DRIVER   This monthly covers much of the same material as R & T, but there is enough unduplicated material to make both publications a monthly "must." Features many excellent photographs. Much newsstands, one-year subscription $5 from C/D Circulation Dept., Portland Place, Boulder, Colorado.

Newspapers

COMPETITION PRESS/AUTOWEEK A 16-page tabloid weekly newspaper devoted entirely to motor sports. Coverage of all major international and U.S. events; many secondary ones (SCCA Regional races, for example). The fastest, best way of getting up-to-date motor-racing news. One-year subscription $9 from Competition Press, 15 Boardman Place, San Francisco, Calif.

Books about Cars

AUTOMOBIL REVUE, Geneva Show Catalog Number. Published in Bern. About $5.00 in this country. Not really a book, but an over-four-hundred-page, soft-cover yearly issue of the Swiss motoring publication *Automobil Revue*. This issue is published to coincide with the annual Geneva automobile show. A complete catalogue, with exhaustive specifications, of almost all the world's automobiles. *Text in French and German,* although an English key to the specifications is included. Many interesting articles and photos.

THE BOOK OF SPORTS CARS   Markmann and Sherwin, Putnam, $15. A solid big (over three hundred pages) book, containing excellent photos, background and description on just about every sports car most enthusiasts have ever heard of. Includes sections on car builders and famous drivers. An invaluable reference.

GUIDES in the MODERN SPORTS CAR SERIES. Sports Car Press, Ltd., New York, $1.95 each. Each book (soft covers, 128 pages, pocket-size) is a guide to one make of car. Makes include Austin-Healey, Corvette, Jaguar, MG, Mercedes, Porsche, Triumph, and VW. All interesting (particularly if you own the make covered) though, since they are all by different authors they vary considerably in approach and detail. Most include history and development, specifications, tuning, etc. Photographs.

THE SPORTS CAR—ITS DESIGN AND PERFORMANCE. Colin Campbell, Robert Bentley, Inc., $8.50. A first-rate technical book by an expert. Not about specific cars, but rather on the various components common to all sports cars: engine, brakes, chassis, etc. Has an excellent glossary of technical terms.

THE SPORTS CAR ENGINE, ITS TUNING AND MODIFICATION. Colin Campbell, Robert Bentley, $8.50. Over 300 pages of basic information about tuning sports car engines, both theory and practice. Plus much information on modifying such engines for increased power. Covers camshafts, supercharging, fuel injection, etc.

THE WORLD'S RACING AND SPORTS CARS Twite, Doubleday, $3.95. A small book that is a useful and detailed collection of some ninety of the world's high-performance cars. About two thirds are sports cars, the rest Formula and touring machines. A photo of each, plus a page of background and specifications to accompany it. Originally published in Great Britain.

Books on Driving

GUIDE TO COMPETITION DRIVING Paul O'Shea, Sports Car Press, Ltd., $1.95. A clear and expert book on how to drive in competition, unexcelled in simplicity and readability, by one of the country's top drivers. Full details on cornering, down-shifting, bank and straightaway driving. Useful even for those who do not want to compete but simply want to drive well. Photos and diagrams.

THE RACING DRIVER Denis Jenkinson, Robert Bentley, Inc., $5. One of England's best-known racing journalists on the theory and practice of road-racing. Interesting not only technically, but for some of Jenkinson's psychological insights as well. Also in paperback.

SPORTS CAR AND COMPETITION DRIVING. Paul Frere, Robert Bentley, $5.00. Among Frere's many credentials as a writer about driving is the fact that he was co-winner at Le Mans in 1960. A noted motoring writer as well as racer, his Sports Car and Competition Driving is among the best on the subject. A how-to-do-it book by a real pro.

THE TECHNIQUE OF MOTOR RACING Piero Taruffi, Robert Bentley, Inc., $8.50. Expensive but superb. Taruffi is an Italian driver (now retired) of nearly world-championship caliber, particularly in sports cars. He is an engineer and designer as well. A very detailed text —part analysis and part how-to-do-it—with many photos and drawings.

Miscellaneous Books

ADVENTURE ON WHEELS John Fitch with W. Nolan, Putnam, $4.50. A racing autobiography by one of America's foremost drivers. Spans Fitch's career from his first race in an MG-TC in 1949 to his experiences in the Corvette SS at Sebring in 1957—his second year as Corvette team manager. Contains much personal inside information on the Mercedes team, the famous American Cunningham team, Le Mans, and other fascinating topics. Since Fitch has competed in nearly all of the top sports car races in the world, this is a unique book. Photographs.

AUTOMOBILE YEAR Edited by Guichard, $12.50. English edition of a Swiss-published annual. Contains very little that is directly about American sports car racing (with the exception of a full Sebring report), but is a detailed and exciting résumé of the year's international Grand Prix and sports car races. Each race is covered in detail—starting position, lap charts, etc. Also contains articles—historical, critical, technical—of general automotive interest. Handsomely printed; includes marvelous photographs. *Automobile Year* is published in late winter or early spring.

DESIGN AND BEHAVIOUR OF THE RACING CAR. Stirling Moss and Laurence Pomeroy, William Kimber (London), $10.50. A most unusual book—a collaboration between top-flight driver and top-flight automotive designer. Almost wholly about Formula I Grand Prix cars— and the relationship between their design and driving characteristics. The cars are those that Moss has driven: Cooper, BRM, Maserati, Mercedes, Vanwall, Lotus. Rather technical, seldom emotional, wholly fascinating to the knowledgeable.

KINGS OF THE ROAD Ken Purdy, Bantam Books; 50¢. Purdy is one of the best writers—if not *the* best writer—in English on automobiles. While there's little in *Kings of the Road* that has to do directly with American sports car racing, there's a great deal to please anyone interested in great races, great cars, and great drivers, mostly of the past. Such topics as Bugatti, Nuvolari, Mercedes, MG, Alfa Romeo, Bentley, and the Vanderbilt Cup are brought to life as only Purdy can do it. Photographs.

OMNIBUS OF SPEED   Edited by Beaumont and Nolan, Putnam, $5.95. An unparalleled anthology, packed with articles (and some fiction) about motor-racing, mostly international. Authors include some notable writers and some notable drivers: Randall Jarrell, Ken Purdy, Denis Jenkinson, John Fitch, Stirling Moss, Masten Gregory, Rudolph Caracciola. Much background on motor sports as a whole, some on U.S. topics: Corvette, Formula III, drivers Shelby, Gregory and Phil Hill. Try and put it down!

SPORTS CAR RALLIES, TRIALS AND GYMKHANAS   Hebb and Peck, Channel Press, $6. The "rallyist's Bible"—and a readable and useful one it is. Contains a wealth of down-to-earth about winning rallies (and other non-racing events) by an expert pair. Also contains some general information about sports car racing. Revised in 1960.

GLOSSARY

Note: numbers in parentheses refer to pages in this book where more detailed explanations or discussion of terms may be found.

ACCUS   Automobile Competition Committee for the United States: U.S. FIA representative.

ALFIN   Trade name for a highly effective type of bimetallic brake drum. (84)

BALANCING   Removing or adding weight to moving engine parts to permit smoother, more reliable high-speed operation. (95)

BHP   Abbreviation for "brake horsepower."

BLACK-FLAG   To signal a car to stop at its pit by means of the black flag. (37)

BLIP   Racing slang for a quick jab at the accelerator to raise rpm. momentarily. Part of down-shift procedure. (48)

BLOWN   Slang for "supercharged," as in "blown engine."

BORE   Cylinder diameter. To "bore out" is to increase displacement by increasing cylinder diameter. "Big bore" is used to describe engines of considerable displacement—say, over three liters.

BRAKE FADE   A condition that reduces or nullifies the effectiveness of brakes. (84)

BRAKE HORSEPOWER   The measure of the horsepower actually delivered by an engine.

CAMSHAFT   A rotating shaft bearing cams that actuate the valves in an engine. (77)

CASTROL   Trade name for a widely used line of racing oils and lubricants.

CC   Abbreviation for "cubic centimeter(s)"—1/1000 of a liter.

CHICANE   A pair or series of very tight and deceptive turns. Usually set up artificially at an unexpected point on the course.

CHIEF STEWARD   Head official at racing events. (33)

CONCOURS D'ÉLÉGANCE   A stationary competition in which cars are judged on maintenance, cleanliness, and taste.

CONNECTING ROD   The rod that transmits the motion of the piston to the crankshaft.

CORNERING   The technique or manner of driving in turns. (45)

CRASH BOX   A non-synchronized gearbox. (82)

CSCC   California Sports Car Club.

CUBIC INCH   The American measure of displacement. 61 cubic inches are equal to 1 liter. (22)

CUNA   Abbreviation for the commission that sets Italian automotive technical standards: *Commissione Unificazione e Normalizzazione Autoveicoli.*

DE DION   A type of rear suspension. (88)

DIN   Abbreviation for the German set of automotive technical standards: *Deutsche Industrie Normen.*

DISPLACEMENT   The measure of engine size. (22)

DOUBLE-CLUTCHING   A technique used in shifting gears. (48)

DOWNDRAFT CARBURETOR   A carburetor designed so that air is drawn down through it into the engine. Usually located above the engine.

DOWN-SHIFT   Shifting from a higher gear to a lower one—for example, from fourth to third. (46)

DRIFT   A cornering technique in which all four wheels have only partial adhesion. (51)

DRIVE SHAFT   The rotating shaft that transmits power from transmission to differential, or in the case of cars with rear-mounted transmissions, from engine to transmission.

DUAL-PURPOSE   Used to describe a car that can be used practically for both competition and touring. (93)

DUAL-THROAT   Used to describe a carburetor with two throats that can feed two manifolds individually. Also called "dual-choke." (80)

ESSES   One or more linked turns.

FALSE GRID   An off-the-course area where cars are positioned prior to a race. It duplicates the real grid at the starting line. (30)

FEATHERING   Very delicate, precise use of the accelerator.

FIA   Fédération Internationale de l'Automobile—the international governing body of motor sport. (18)

FISHTAIL   A partial loss of control of a car in which its rear end swings from side to side in a series of short skids.

FLIP   Slang for overturning a car.

FORMULA CARS   Specific classes of all-out road-racing single-seater cars. Displacement limits for some of the important Formulas are: *Formula I*—Since 1966, 3000 cc. unsupercharged, 1500 cc, supercharged. International.
Formula SCCA—three separate single-seater open-wheel classifications. Formula A allows engines to 3000 cc., Formula B to 1600 cc., Formula C to 1100 cc. U.S. only.
Formula Vee—Relatively stock Volkswagen engines that push a car much of whose running gear is also VW. (28). U.S. only.

FORMULA LIBRE   Literally, "free formula," which means anything that can be put on the track can compete.

FOUR STROKE   Used to describe an engine in which there is one power stroke of the piston to every three non-power strokes. The strokes in the four-stroke cycle, in order, are *intake, compression, power,* and *exhaust.* The common type of automobile engine, also referred to as "four-cycle."

FUEL INJECTION   A system for getting fuel to the cylinders without first mixing it with air in a carburetor. (81)

GRAND PRIX   A championship race for Formula I cars. Often used loosely to describe any big race.

GRID   A pattern on which cars are positioned for a standing start. (41)

GT   Abbreviation for "*Gran Turismo*" or "Grand Touring."

GYMKHANA   An event, usually

low-speed, in which drivers compete in skill and agility at handling their cars. (60)

HILL CLIMB   A timed event in which cars compete, one at a time, on a course laid out on an uphill stretch of road. (62)

ICE RACE   Race held on a circuit laid out on a frozen lake or pond. (61)

IN-LINE   Used to describe an engine in which the cylinders are positioned in a single line. (76)

INBOARD BRAKE   Any brake not located at the wheel. (85)

INFIELD   The area encompassed by a road circuit.

JET   A nozzle from which gasoline is fed into the air stream in the carburetor.

LE MANS START   A method of starting a race in which drivers are positioned across the track from their cars before the starting signal. (41)

LINE   The path a car follows on the course, particularly through a corner. (52)

LISCA   Long Island Sports Car Association.

LITER   A metric measure of volume; about 10 per cent larger than a quart. One liter equals 61 cubic inches. (22)

LIVE AXLE   The type of rear axle found on all American cars and many European ones, in which rotating axle shafts are enclosed in a rigid casing that extends from one rear wheel to the other. (88)

MAGNETO   A type of electrical generator. (82)

MANIFOLD   The unit of pipes that carries air/fuel mixture from carburetor to intake ports (*intake* manifold) or exhaust gas from exhaust ports to exhaust pipes (*exhaust* manifold).

MARQUE   French for "make"—as in "make of car."

MICHELIN X   A French tire with steel cords, particularly renowned for its adhesion on wet surfaces.

MODIFIED   Used to describe a car that is not stock or as purchased. (93)

NASCAR   National Association for Stock Car Auto Racing—the organization that sanctions most American stock car racing.

OIL RADIATOR   A separate radiator through which engine oil is circulated and cooled. (82)

OPPOSED   Used to describe an engine in which cylinders are opposite each other (the Porsche engine, for example). (76)

OUTBOARD BRAKE   Any brake at the conventional location at the wheel. (85)

OVERSQUARE   Said of an engine with a bore greater than its stroke. (112)

PADDOCK   An enclosed area reserved for contestants, their crews and their cars at a race. (30)

PITS   The track-side area at which cars are serviced during a race. More loosely, "pits" is sometimes stretched to include the paddock. (29)

PRANG   Racing slang for a collision.

PRODUCTION   Used to describe a car that is more or less mass-produced and to which major modifications have not been made. (93)

PSI   Pounds per Square Inch—a measure of air pressure (as in tires, for example).

PUMP FUEL   Commercially available automotive gasoline.

PUSH RODS   Reciprocating rods that transmit the action of the cams to valves (usually overhead). A "push rod engine" is thus one that has overhead valves but not overhead camshafts. (77)

QUICK-CHANGE REAR END   A differential in which some of the gears are readily accessible so that rear-axle gear ratios can be quickly and easily altered.

RACK AND PINION   A type of steering gear—fast, simple, and direct—in which a pinion gear on the lower end of the steering column meshes with a rack (gear teeth cut along a straight edge) connected with the front wheels.

RALLY   An event in which cars compete at covering a specified course—usually on public roads —at specified average speeds. (60)

RATIO   The relative speed at which two or more meshed gears revolve.

REVS   Slang for *Revolutions Per Minute* (rpm.).

ROCKER ARM   A pivoted arm that transmits motion from a push rod or cam to a valve. (77)

ROLL BAR   A protective device to keep a car from crushing its driver in the event of its overturning. (66)

RPM   Revolutions Per Minute—the speed at which an engine turns. (47)

SAE   Abbreviation for the organization that sets American automotive technical standards: the *Society of Automotive Engineers.*

SANCTION   Approval or authorization of an event by one or more of the sport's governing bodies: FIA, USAC, SCCA, etc. (18)

SCCA   Sports Car Club of America.

SCUDERIA   Literally, Italian for "stable." A racing team or group.

SHUNT   Slang. To bump or shove another car during a race.

SHUT-OFF POINT   The point at which a driver must begin to reduce speed preparatory to taking a corner. (47)

SIDE-DRAFT CARBURETOR   A carburetor so designed that air is drawn through it horizontally. Usually located alongside the engine.

SLIDE   A controlled skid. (49)

SLIP STREAM   The partial vacuum created behind a speeding car. "To slip-stream" is to move one's own car into the vacuum behind a competitor's car, thus taking advantage of the pull of this additional motive force. (45)

SPECIAL   A one-of-a-kind or few-of-a-kind racing car built by an individual or small organization. (134)

SPIN   An out-of-control slide, usually of 180° or more, in which the car is wrenched off its proper line and often completely stopped.

STAGE   A specific degree of tuning for higher horsepower. A hypothetical engine might turn out 100 bhp. in its stock form, 105 bhp. in Stage I tune, 110 in Stage II tune, 120 bhp. in Stage III tune.

STOCK   As put together by the manufacturer; not modified.

STRAIGHT PIPES   A direct exhaust

system that does not include a muffler.

STROKE   The distance a piston travels between its highest and lowest points.

SUPERCHARGER   A compressor for charging an engine with more fuel-air mixture than can be charged by atmospheric pressure alone. (80)

SWING AXLE   A type of rear suspension in which the rear axle shafts are pivoted at the differential. (90)

SYNCHROMESH   A system of mechanisms in the gearbox for synchronizing the relative speeds of gears that are to be meshed. (82)

TACHOMETER   An instrument that indicates engine speed (rpm.).

TORQUE   A twisting force.

TORSION BAR   A bar that, when twisted, supplies the same effect as a spring. (86)

TUNE   Slang for the degree of efficiency at which an engine performs. A highly-tuned engine is one that is delivering its maximum potential.

TWIN CAMS   Slang for two camshafts in racing parlance; double overhead camshafts.

TWO-STROKE   Used to describe a type of engine that has only two piston strokes in its cycle. Widely used in scooters, motorcycles, and also in a few cars (Saab, DKW, etc.).

UNSPRUNG WEIGHT   That part of a car's total weight that rests not on the springs but directly on the road: wheels, tires, frequently brakes, differential, etc. (87)

UPSHIFT   Shifting from a lower gear to a higher one—for example, from third to fourth.

USAC   United States Automobile Club—an organization that sanctions professional sports car racing in this country, as well as much other racing. (19)

VALVE FLOAT   An undesirable condition that occurs at high rpm. when valve springs cannot keep valves in contact with their actuating mechanisms. (79)

WEIGHT DISTRIBUTION   The way in which a car's weight is divided between its front and rear wheels. Usually expressed in percentages: 45/55, for example. (75)

WHEEL BASE   The distance between front and rear wheels, as measured from the center of the wheels.

WHITWORTH   The British system of nut and bolt sizes.

WISHBONE   A wishbone- or A-shaped suspension arm. (119)

WORKS   British term for "factory." A "works team" is a team of cars entered and supported by their manufacturer.